Praise for *Don't Retire, Get Inspired*

"An inspiring and compelling story of how life can be renewed by good works."

—**Scott Turow**
Attorney and author of seven best-selling novels

"An incredible journey of passion and compassion. Mr. and Mrs. Nogaj set an example of how you can give back and certainly nourish the notion that you are not done with your life after retirement. Their example is one to definitely follow. A must-read for people of good will."

—**Luis E. Pelayo**
Founder and President
Hispanic Council of Chicago

"A life well-lived, someone said, is to have children, plant a tree, and write a book. Dick Nogaj has not only done all three, but so much, much more. And in keeping with his commitments, he was willing to spend the time and effort to share an inkling of how much more it really was. This is a story that keeps on telling of a life lived to the fullest. What a great read!"

—**Dr. Wayne Robinson**
Minister
All Faiths Congregation, Fort Myers, Florida

"Many couples talk about wanting to make a difference in the lives of others less fortunate than them. Dick and Florence Nogaj did more than talk. Their story is an inspiring example of 'making a difference' through love, hard work, and personal risk-taking."

—**Alan J. Hollenbeck, P.E.**
President/CEO
RJN Group, Wheaton, Illinois

"'That's too bad' is a common remark some people use when confronted with poverty and despair. Not the Nogajs. Dick and Florence have a contagious gumption when it comes to tackling a situation in spite of sheer challenges, risks, and discomforts. They have received much and want to give back by working with those in need. Reading this book may give you the courage to say, 'Perhaps I can do something like that, too!'"

—**Linda C. Fuller**
Co-Founder
Habitat for Humanity International and
the Fuller Center for Housing

"*Don't Retire, Get Inspired* is an awe-inspiring journey of two people in love with each other, their family, their fellow human beings, and their God. A must-read for all who have an abiding faith in the goodness of the human spirit and in love itself."

—**William J. Carroll**
President
Benedictine University, Springfield College in Illinois

"*Don't Retire, Get Inspired* should be required reading for every 'Baby Boomer' contemplating 'retirement.' To Richard and Florence Nogaj, 'retirement' is a misnomer for a beautiful time of life in which great spiritual growth is possible with incredible dividends of satisfaction and inspiration. In this fine book, Richard Nogaj tells an inspirational story of how spiritual growth, the desire to bring a life partnership to new levels, and dedication to a cause greater than themselves can be translated into a call to action improving the lives of many people in the farming community of Immokalee, Florida."

—**Dr. John H. Fitch**
Director
Sustaining Tomorrow Today Project
Florida Gulf Coast University

"Richard Nogaj shows that we don't have to go to the Third World to go to the Third World. The same oppressive poverty that he found in the Dominican Republic, he found in his own backyard—and this is the story of what he did about it. This book deserves two thumbs up!"

—**Tony Campolo**
Professor Emeritus of Sociology,
Eastern University

"A moving story of a courageous couple that dared to dream the impossible."

—**Ronald J. Sider**
President
Evangelicals for Social Action

Don't Retire, Get Inspired

One Couple's Extraordinary
Journey to Make a Difference

DON'T RETIRE,
GET INSPIRED

DICK NOGAJ

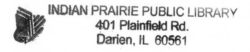

WinePress WP Publishing

WinePress Publishing (PO Box 428, Enumclaw, WA 98022) functions only as book publisher. As such, the ultimate design, content, editorial accuracy, and views expressed or implied in this work are those of the author.

Scripture taken from the *New King James Version*. Copyright © 1979, 1980, 1983 by Thomas Nelson, Inc. Used by permission. All rights reserved.

ISBN 13: 978-1-60615-021-4
ISBN 10: 1-60615-021-9
Library of Congress Catalog Card Number: 2009934535

Printed in South Korea.

To Florence.

*"For where two or three are gathered together in My name,
I am there in the midst of them."*
—Matthew 18:20

With my wife Florence in my life I always knew that the Lord was not only there, but was calling us to love each other in a special way that would help make this world a better place. You have helped me be a better person, and your steady, encouraging love and willingness to enter into a spiritual partnership with me enabled us to take this special risk-filled journey to make the difference in the lives of others.

You have my care and my respect, and you are my love.

CONTENTS

ACKNOWLEDGMENTS

THE LIST OF PEOPLE that have touched the lives of Florence and me over our incredible journey during the last fifteen years is lengthy and practically countless. So, if you don't find your name here, please know that I am grateful for our encounter. Even if you're not listed here, you may be mentioned in the book by name—now you may have to read it!

First, I thank Florence. Not only did she take this journey with me starting in 1994, providing endless support, patience, and the loving attitude of a true soulmate, she endured with me over the last two years to help me write this book about our journey. She took dictation, set up "The Book" computer files, and instructed me how to "take it from there." She is very special, which is why this book is dedicated to her.

I want to also thank all those who participated in researching and writing this book. From the beginning Rev. Dr. Wayne Robinson got me started in the right direction with a review of earlier outlines, chapters, and content. Thank you, Wayne, for a great start. Annie Estlund helped with early ideas and a review of early chapters. Thank you so much. And thank you, Joan and Segundo Velasquez, for your feedback. I am also grateful for early input from Dr. John Fitch and his wife, Jean. I appreciate your input and direction during the writing of the first few chapters as well as your warm, heartfelt encouragement during our work in Immokalee when you brought your class from Florida Gulf Coast University to become involved in the Jubilation experience.

Deeply felt thanks to my ever-loving sister, Barbara, and her husband, Mike Norris, who always listened attentively without ever losing interest in our work. Although my mom passed on just before I started the book, I want to thank her for her unwavering love and support that she gave to both Florence and me during our journey. Thanks for the support and encouragement from my dear lifelong friend, Len LaPasso and his wife, Virginia.

Thanks to another friend, Bob Teichart, who steered me on a very special course when he suggested a developmental editor to assist me when I finally got the material down on the page. Bob recommended Kelly James-Enger, who was exactly what I needed to help edit and prepare the final manuscript. Kelly made this book possible by bringing to it her wit, her experience, and her ability to capture and retain my voice.

Some of the most encouraging advice I received was from author Scott Turow, who told me that our story needed to be told, and to concentrate on "getting it down and fixing it up afterwards." Thank you for your interest, ideas, suggestions, and encouragement along the way that helped me to stay on course to write and finish the book. Scott also suggested attending the "Write to Publish Conference" in Wheaton, Illinois, which turned out to be great advice. There we met Athena Dean and later selected her WinePress Group as our publisher. I am grateful to everyone at WinePress for their competence, patience, and understanding.

I want to extend a very special thanks to Chuck DiGiovanni, our accountant, and Alan Garfield, our attorney, who guided me and kept me on the right track from the beginning of RJN Group, Inc. as well as during the extraordinary journey that Florence and I have taken over the last fifteen years.

A number of people played essential roles during our Habitat work in DuPage County and I appreciate their work. Attorney Steve Alderman assisted with a multitude of closings. Vicki Broberg, a member of the original Founders Council, and Charlotte O'Connell have both been stabilizing influences throughout the years. Jessie Arzola served faithfully as a family mentor; Sandy Bergeson donated her musical talents at several DuPage Habitat events; and Woodie Bessler stepped up when the "going got tough."

All of the families we worked with at DuPage Habitat for Humanity in Illinois and the Harvest for Humanity families in Florida are special. But among them are also "VSPs," or very special families. Both Florence and I would like to express our love to them; while we thought we were giving to them, they were giving back so much more to Florence and me. The Habitat families of Alex and Elsie Vela, Caroline and Alejandro Zavala, Chi and Kim Nguyen, Manual and Guadalupe Fernandez, Norma Tee, Christine Sena, and Francisco and Teodomira Aparicio are VSPs.

In Immokalee, Florida, the families that have especially touched us include Jacob and Carmelita Lopez, Elizabeth DeLaRosa, Steve Perez, Juan and Martha Anzualda, Brian Boudreaux, Tom Carmichael, Gloria Dominguez, Rafael and Maria Espinoza, Yvette Fleurisma and Lacariere Herrard, Francisco and Grisel Gaspar, Adan and Anita Hernandez, Marco and Elda Perez-Hernandez, Bobby and Grace Hudson, Marie Jean, Jerry and Diana Kennedy, Graclie Milfort and her son, Max Surin, Michael and Jennifer MacMenamin, Désilus Nicolas, Dieutafait Pierre, and Froylan and Carmen Resendiz.

I extend my appreciation to Will Grosch for his professional expertise and personal attention and thank Chris Shields and Christina Schwinn for their legal assistance.

In Fort Myers, Florence and I were grateful for the initial help we received from Richard Shera, Jr. for the Jubilation project. Thank you also to Mr. Abdul'Haq Muhammed for his efforts to bring new opportunities to the children in Jubilation.

Our journey with Harvest for Humanity was also made special by our friendships with Tony Lombardo, Ann Cotner, and Steve and Lydia Sherman. I also want to thank Buddy Walker for his help in developing and maintaining our Harvest website.

One gentleman, Ron Davis, worked tirelessly with Florence and me on grant-writing efforts. We both deeply appreciate his encouragement and tenacity in this important work. The owners of American Heritage Title Company, Bill Banyasz, his wife, Janet, and their son, Bill, appreciated the concept of Jubilation and provided critical, much-needed participation to help close on the homes.

We thoroughly enjoyed working with Pat Shapiro, who helped develop our special blueberry label and design our much-talked about mascot, "Ponce de la Blueberry." Our time with you was "fruitful," and we thank you for your creative work. I thank Bernie Kleina for his steady guidance during some of our Habitat work and Ricardo Skerrett for his important contribution to the welfare of farm worker families during our Harvest work.

I'm also grateful for the friends from the 60s that I was able to reconnect with forty years later. They still worship together at the Religious Education Community (REC) and include Warren and Margaret Roth, Bob Russo, Frank and Kay Goetz,

Paul and Eileen Lefort, Rosie Dixon, Fran Holtzman, Ruth Riha, Joe and Connie Sunderhaus, and Bob Elliot. Thank you for your friendship and support.

A very special person entered my life just before I met Florence. He has passed on, but Ed Younger was a pillar of support in tough times and was always there for me when I needed him. Thank you, Ed, for so much care.

I also want to thank my adult children, Debbie, Tom, and John, and their families, and Florence's adult children, Johanna and Jennifer, and their families—for their love.

FOREWORD

I RECENTLY REREAD SCHOLAR Paul Loeb's book, *Soul of a Citizen*. Its subtitle is *Living with Conviction in a Cynical Time*. That could be a subtitle for the book you are about to read. Because if there is anything that comes through, over and over in *Don't Retire—Get Inspired!*, it is that Dick and Flo Nogaj have deep and abiding conviction for the "living of these days."

In the late 20th century, Flo and Dick, living well in Chicago, took the money from the sale of the company Dick had built before he met Flo, and together they invested it in an incredible concept that became an amazing community. Today, Jubilation even has a university at its center—all in a community of almost 100 houses built and enabled by Flo and Dick.

The dream they worked to realize was a unique kind of affordable housing . . . beautiful homes facing each other, with sidewalks that invite neighborliness. They fought for those with work records, but without good credit history. They went to bat at banks for those who had never had a bank loan before in their lives.

And built into the community were guidelines to insure property values would be maintained and stability would always be present. In the end, their dream became the reality of several hundred, mostly first-time homeowners.

Dick and Flo's willingness to do that came out of an earlier time in their lives of commitment to causes that made a difference—the civil rights movement, Habitat for Humanity, educational excellence—and all while Dick was building a national corporation of engineers. They each had a faith that was more than shibboleths . . . more than mere words repeated over and over. Theirs was a spiritual commitment that eventuated into a unique kind of civic engagement.

Best-selling author Paul Hawkens writes that it wasn't until the middle of the eighteenth century and the rise of the abolitionist movement that a group of people organized themselves to help people they would never know, and from whom they would never receive direct or indirect benefit.

Dick and Flo knew no one in Immokalee, Florida, a "Third World country" next door to Naples, Florida, in one of the richest counties in America. But when they learned about Immokalee's challenges and needs, they determined to provide a unique kind of affordable housing to people they didn't know, with no profit in it for themselves.

That story, plus so much more, is told in this book in wonderful detail. Their relationship was tested, their best efforts to help at times rejected, and their self-confidence challenged to the bone. But they kept at it, and now they are able to tell the story, and what a story it is.

Initially, I planned to read the first and last chapters, and then scan the rest to read more closely at a later time. I found myself unable to put it down.

I know that will be your experience as well, when you engage this modern-day story of what it means to put a deep commitment to helping others into practice, when it costs you nearly everything you had saved and worked for.

Dick and Flo not only talk the talk, but as *Don't Retire* tells so entrancingly, they have most certainly walked the walk. I envy you getting to read this for the first time. You'll be inspired, engaged, and amazed.

—Dr. Wayne Robinson
Minister
All Faiths Unitarian Congregation
Fort Myers, Florida

PART I
EARLY YEARS

Chapter One

DO YOU BELIEVE
IN ANGELS?

AS MY CAR APPROACHED the intersection at Naperville Road and Willow Avenue near downtown Wheaton, a western suburb of Chicago, something to my right caught my eye. I noticed a man motioning to me while approaching the passenger window of my car. Was he a hitchhiker? In the suburbs, it was unusual to see anyone hitching a ride, and this middle-aged man was well-groomed, blond hair neatly combed, and wearing a suit and tie with a dark overcoat. In one hand he held a large black umbrella. Why would *he* be hitching a ride?

It was March 1998, and I had not picked up a hitchhiker in at least thirty years. Yet I rolled down the window to see what he wanted. He nodded and asked, with a slight British accent, "Do you know where Saint Daniel the Prophet Catholic Church is located?"

Then I heard myself say, "Sure I do. I'm going that way. Get in and I will take you there." I had no anxiety about letting a stranger into my car. Something about him seemed safe. And after all, I reasoned, it was a drizzly day and I just couldn't leave him there. I had to make a right turn anyway to get to my destination—a fast food restaurant to grab a quick lunch. The church was in the same direction and not out of my way.

We talked a little on the way, and he told me he was associated with a Christian ministry in South Africa and was looking for a contact at Saint Daniel's. I pointed out that as it was a weekday and around lunchtime, he might not find the person he was looking for. "Not to worry," he said, relaxing against the passenger seat.

When he asked about my work, I told him that during the last few years, my wife Florence and I had started two not-for-profit organizations in Wheaton—a corporate foundation and an affiliate for Habitat for Humanity.

We came to a stop at a street near the church. "Drop me off here," he said, motioning at the long sidewalk that led from the curb to the church entrance. He opened the car door, but before he climbed out, he turned to me and said, "God has something very big planned for you. Many will try to convince you that you will not be able to accomplish it. You should persevere," he said. "Listen to God's calling and proceed when His plan is unveiled."

I stared as he climbed out of the car and began to stroll up the sidewalk toward the church. He turned his head, telling me not to wait and that he would be okay. He waved, opening his black umbrella as a light rain began to fall and I drove away.

A few blocks away at the nearby take-out restaurant, I sat in my car eating a chicken sandwich, asking myself what had just happened. I'd parked facing a hedge of bushes that was about twenty feet from the sidewalk running along a busy street. Through an opening in the bushes, I was surprised to see my hitchhiker on the sidewalk. He was smiling, closed umbrella tilted against his shoulder, a gleeful step in his stride that reminded me of the famous scene from *Singing in the Rain*, when

Gene Kelly splashes his way along the street. As my hitchhiker walked past the bushes, he disappeared from view.

I wondered how to tell Florence what had happened. Would she think I had "lost it"? I knew I would get an understanding response from her, but for some reason, I hesitated. We hadn't had a vacation for a while and were looking forward to a week in Florida next month. I decided to wait and tell her then.

I finished my sandwich lost in thought. Instead of hurrying back to the office like I usually did, I became distracted. I found myself thinking of my favorite movie, *It's a Wonderful Life*. I'd first seen it as a child in the 1940s and ever since then, I had harbored a secret desire to build a Bailey Park, a community of new homes for people who would never have owned their own home without the compassionate help of the savings and loan president, George Bailey. Even as a little boy, I had always been inspired by the story of how many lives one person can change for the better.

As a kid, I developed an intense desire for financial security. It wasn't that I wanted to be rich when I grew up, but I knew I didn't want to have to worry about money. Growing up on the northwest side of Chicago, nearing the end of the Great Depression, my parents didn't have a lot of money. My dad was a machinist who eventually worked his way up to become a quality control supervisor for a precision parts machine shop. My mom was a homemaker who occasionally worked part-time administrative jobs. They couldn't afford to give me an allowance, and I always hated not having any money in my pocket.

Starting early at about eight years old, I rummaged for pop bottles so I could return them for the deposit. A few years later one of my uncles gave me a hand-me-down bike and I got a paper route so I could buy a new bike. From the age of twelve, I worked at the bingo halls, waiting on tables for tips every Friday night. At fifteen years old, I was working the night shift in a machine shop saving money to go to college.

But my parents' love and attention had a greater effect on me than an allowance ever could have. My father was self-taught, and read the classics in his spare time. He taught me to play cribbage when I was eight or nine years old, which helped develop my love of math. My mom taught me to think independently, and not to accept everything I learned at school as absolute truths. She was something of an enigma—while she never volunteered at a social agency, she believed in fairness and equal rights, especially for the underdog. By her example, I learned about treating others with kindness and compassion, and about learning to be fair but firm.

What my folks may have lacked in money, they more than made up for with their love for and belief in education. That was instilled in me, and I was always encouraged to do my best in school and to aim for college.

My parents weren't the only ones encouraging me to excel. My mom came from a family of eight, all of whom lived nearby, so I had lots of aunts and uncles who always encouraged me later to achieve whatever I could. Some of my favorite memories are of the old-fashioned "garage parties" my grandmother would host behind her two-story home in the Cragin neighborhood of Chicago. The polka music blared, the beer flowed like water, and family and neighbors all joined in as we danced the night away.

As the first-born male growing up in the 40s in a Catholic Chicago neighborhood, there was an implicit expectation for me to become a priest. This possibility waned with time. I had a girlfriend in third grade and every grade thereafter—and not always the same girl. I never really stopped loving girls, but I did make a decision to give up—on the priesthood.

What I didn't give up was my desire to personally escape poverty and my willingness to work hard to do so. After graduating from high school, I earned engineering degrees from the Illinois Institute of Technology in Chicago. In the years after, I married, started a family, and focused on building my career and taking care of my family. When I was twenty-four, though, I met someone who would broaden my horizons—Gene Boivin.

Gene and I worked together at an environmental company near Chicago in Melrose Park. Gene was a tall, lanky guy a few years older than me who was deeply committed to his religious beliefs and to changing the world. He was determined to get me to join his cause and to participate in a spiritual retreat called a Cursillo, short for *Cursillo de Christiandad*, which translates to "short course in Christianity." The weekend was promoted as a life-changing experience.

In November 1963, I finally gave in and attended the retreat. About fifty of us arrived on a Friday evening at the Cursillo Center near downtown Chicago, had dinner, and attended an introductory session before we retired to our sleeping quarters. On Saturday and Sunday, we attended five group presentations each day. Before the first session, we were assigned to eight different tables in the large conference room; each table had one experienced team member who gave a presentation to the group.

The speakers made presentations about Christian action, faith, love, and civil rights based on their real-life experiences about the subject. Roland Sebrie was the team member at my table. An African-American in his mid-sixties, he was medium height and build, with short graying hair. As Roland spoke about his personal experiences with hatred—growing up as a black man in the South with first-hand encounters with the Ku Klux Klan—no man in the room was able to keep a dry eye.

On Sunday evening, the retreat came to an end. We were dismissed to a large room, only to be surprised by hundreds of "Cursillistas," former Cursillo attendees. We participated in an Ultreya (an evening meeting of Cursillistas) closing ceremony where we all sang *De Colores*, the theme song of Cursillo, which welcomed all of us to our new life.

I hadn't expected to have such an inspiring and personally emotional experience at the Cursillo. Beforehand, I had taken my family to church but I didn't have a strong spiritual life. The Cursillo solidified my personal relationship with God. It softened my judgmental attitude toward others and fostered understanding, and I began to more easily love and respect others who didn't share my views. Actually after the Cursillo, I just couldn't believe how much everyone else had changed!

I was also profoundly moved by meeting and learning more about Roland. He was the first African-American man I had really gotten to know, and he and I became good friends, visiting each other's homes and getting to know each other's families. It was my relationship with him that inspired me to join the civil rights movement. Eventually I became a member of the Southern Christian Leadership Conference, and I would march, pray, and sing with Dr. Martin Luther King, Jr.

I was there during the summer of 1966 when, on a march in Chicago, gun shots rang out and all of us marchers hit the pavement. After a short time, we were given the "all clear" and the march proceeded. I prayed for courage as we all sang "Ain't Gonna Let Nobody Turn Us Around." After that experience, I trained to become a marshal for subsequent marches in Chicago, where my assignment would be to help keep order. For the next five years, when I wasn't working or with my family, I was working with Gene, Roland, and others to change the world.

In 1968, both Dr. King and Bobby Kennedy were assassinated. For many of us in the civil rights movement, it was the "Day the Music Died." It meant that whites and blacks would enter different spheres in the struggle for justice. The civil rights movement shifted from nonviolence with both white and black participation to a more aggressive Black Power movement dominated by blacks. The others continued to work for justice through organizations that advocated fair housing, equal employment, equal education, and civil rights for all.

While raising their eight children, Gene and his wife, Iris, became missionaries for the Ecumenical Institute in Chicago and continued their work in several parts of the world. Before he and his wife passed on, however, he would visit me when he was in the Chicago area to see how I was answering the call.

But after 1968, I was personally somewhat disillusioned and less hopeful for our country's future. I focused more on my family and building my career. In 1975, I started my own engineering firm, RJN Environmental Associates, Inc. By the early 1990s, the original firm had grown to become RJN Group, Inc. with over one hundred employees, ten offices nationwide and more than twelve million dollars in annual revenues.

Now, as I finished my sandwich that spring day in 1998 after my encounter with the hitchhiker, my thoughts shifted to the work that Florence and I had already done together. We'd worked with Habitat for Humanity and established a Habitat affiliate in DuPage County. We had been deeply involved with

Habitat during the last three years, so what could the hitch-hiker be referring to when he talked about "the plan for the future"? Why would I need to persevere? It was unsettling but I was all too familiar with the feeling of not knowing what might happen next.

Even before I had met Florence, my life had taken some significant turns. My first marriage ended after thirty-three years. I wondered if I would ever find the right partner. I didn't just want a beautiful companion by my side; I wanted a true soulmate, someone who had similar values and a desire to give back. After my divorce, I attended therapy. When my sessions ended, my counselor suggested that I get "moving" again by going to a place called Helpmates, a recovery group for divorced or widowed singles. I remember his words. He said, "She is out there. Now go find her."

I entered the dating scene with reluctance, however. Dating was a different experience than it had been in the 1950s. I went out with several nice women but there were no fireworks. Then one day at Helpmates, I noticed a very attractive, striking woman across the room. When I heard her speak, I knew I wanted to meet her. Her tone was soft but her words were compelling. She talked about her dreams and aspirations without dwelling on any negative things that may have happened in her past.

At the next Helpmates social event, I spotted Florence and quickly asked her to dance. We started off dancing to "Proud Mary", by Credence Clearwater Revival, but we danced to everything from rock to "When I Fall in Love", by Celine Dion and Clive Griffin. When I saw how much she loved to dance, I knew she had possibilities. I asked for her phone number, and called a few days later to ask if I could give her a ride to a Helpmates holiday picnic at a local park. She agreed, and offered to pack a picnic lunch for us. I counted the hours in the meantime.

When I picked her up, Florence greeted me with one of the warmest and most genuine smiles I had ever encountered. She had prepared a perfectly arranged traditional oval-shaped picnic basket with all the trimmings—sandwiches, fruit, and homemade cookies. I was impressed by the time and effort she'd put into our lunch, but I'd soon learn that she never does anything important halfway.

At the park I rented a paddleboat, and we paddled on the water enjoying the green, sloping hills and valleys. The sun was warm, and the air was still except for the occasional sounds of birds. We shared our first kiss under a small bridge, and this time there were definitely fireworks for me. I hoped she felt the same.

Neither of us wanted the day to end. We took a walk through the park, and came upon an empty baseball field and bleachers. We sat on the bleachers and watched a beautiful sunset together, talking about everything from our children to our divorces and how they had changed us. As the sun set, a cool breeze sprang up, and I put my arm around Florence. We talked for a long time about our pasts and our hopes for the future, and agreed that we would take the risk of trusting each other, even if it meant feeling exposed or scared. I told her I thought I was falling in love, and I remember her soft, sweet voice in the darkness answering, "So am I."

Florence wasn't only beautiful inside and out. During the coming months, I learned that she shared my desire to make a difference to help improve the lives of others. That would become our common purpose. I asked her to marry me in September 1993 and we set the wedding date for a year from then.

Florence and I had both been through therapy after our divorces, and we understood many of the emotional wounds we had from our pasts. However, we had no clue how to respond to or heal them, and as a couple we were concerned that they might become obstacles to our future. We were committed to not repeating the same mistakes we had made in the past, but we didn't know how to do that.

We found the book, *Keeping the Love You Find* by Dr. Harville Hendrix, and began working through the exercises on our own. We discovered that each of us had 90 percent of the character traits the other was looking for in a soulmate. This was wonderful, but we both knew that the devil might be in the details—that last 10 percent.

Hendrix's book was about the Imago process, which involves developing and using "wound-healing" tools to build a relationship. At a weekend workshop with the author in San Francisco in 1994, we learned that a real love relationship does not just happen—it takes work. After the workshop, armed with new tools, we came back to Wheaton to live happily ever after, right? Not so fast.

We discovered core feelings that were causing us conflict so we began a search for a local Imago counselor. Leo Dhont taught us how to effectively implement the Imago process and to address those critical issues. For example, one serious issue for many couples is the inability to lovingly resolve conflicts. When a conflict arises, most people tend to choose either "fight" or "flight."

Generally, Florence preferred to flee and I wanted to stay and fight. With Imago, I learned to be calmer, and to use "I" statements instead of "you" statements when I spoke. I worked at keeping my voice low and quiet. Florence worked hard to stay and listen to me instead of ending the discussion or leaving the room. We continued to practice and study, and became more confident that we could use these skills after we got married as well.

But before we could marry, I needed to meet Florence's pastor, John Carrier, of Grace Lutheran Church in the suburb of Western Springs. Florence wanted us to be married by her pastor and friend. I worried about receiving his approval at our first meeting, but I must have passed the test—he married us on September 17, 1994.

About the time we got engaged, Pastor Carrier's wife, Lori, took a new position in a Hispanic neighborhood called "Little City" in Chicago. She was hired as principal of Grace Lutheran School, a private elementary school, with about one hundred students. The administrators and teachers there were struggling to provide an excellent grade school education in a challenging neighborhood beset with poverty. Florence was quickly recruited to join the school's new board of directors and, soon after, was elected president of the board.

Florence worked tirelessly, almost full-time that first year, to help keep the school open. She initiated important programs like tuition "sweat equity" which enabled parents to help with the school's operational and maintenance duties while actively participating in their children's education. She received many deserved accolades, but said later that none was as rewarding as seeing children graduate and go on to succeed in high school and college. As the school continued to impact both its students and neighborhood in a positive way, I saw what a rewarding experience it was for Florence. She had meant it when she said her mission was to help "give back."

As I sat in my car that rainy spring day in 1998, I recalled how Florence and I had started our work together years before—and how it had been an essential element of our love and commitment to each other.

Chapter Two

"Just Laugh—and Keep on Nailing"

THE SAME YEAR I met Florence, I launched the RJN Foundation with the assistance of my accountant, Chuck DiGiovanni, and my attorney, Alan Garfield. Both had been with me since 1975, when I founded my engineering company. With their help, the new RJN Foundation became the "give-back" arm of RJN Group, Inc. While I had been thinking about doing this for quite a while, it was Florence's presence in my life that convinced me it was the right time to do it. The foundation's first project was to help fund Florence's work with the children at Grace School. RJN employees also chipped in with the installation and networking of the school's new computers.

RJN Group had specialized in environmental and municipal infrastructure projects. I had often thought how blessed I was to work in a profession that improved the quality of life for the public. Many of my employees shared that belief; I'd been told more than once, "Dick, what we do at RJN does make a difference." That feeling always made it easier to get up in the morning and greet each day with enthusiasm.

But after almost twenty years, I'd reached a point where I wanted to move on. I felt it was time to begin anew, especially once I'd met Florence. I wasn't as committed to growing the company as I'd been in the past, which didn't seem fair to me or the employees.

Florence and I were both blessed with talent, resources, and the drive to make a difference in other people's lives. Beginning anew might allow us to give back to those who were less fortunate and in a significant way. The RJN Foundation was now established; its mission was to support organizations that were primarily involved in improving the lives of children. That is where Florence and I hoped to start, but until I sold the company, I wouldn't be able to fund the RJN Foundation at any significant level.

Al Hollenbeck, who had joined RJN Group in 1977 shortly after graduating from college, was emerging as a strong and capable leader. I believed that Al could take over the management reins at RJN Group. He had vision and drive, and the RJN principals and staff respected him. During rough times, Al never got discouraged. Instead, he would simply say that we were experiencing the "growing pains" that would help us develop into one of the top 500 *Engineering News Record* (the trade magazine for our industry) firms in the country.

Because of our company's size, expertise, and multiple-office locations, I was looking for a larger firm to buy us out. I was surprised when I learned that Al and several of the other principals—who were already minority stockholders in our closely-held firm—were interested in buying the firm themselves. As we began to explore possible options, we learned more about ESOPs, or Employee Stock Ownership Plans.

We hired an ESOP consultant who conducted several business seminars with the principals and me. Several months into the process, we found a bank that would provide the loan to fund the ESOP trust. If approved, the loan would pay me for the company while the new owners would have seven years to pay off the loan using company profits. The bank insisted that the eight key principals—the largest shareholders positioned to become the managing partners—enter into an agreement requiring them to guarantee their personal assets to purchase the company. This requirement was a challenge to everyone's commitment but it had to be met.

It was at this point that a business consultant suggested that a "bonding experience" might build a higher level of trust among the prospective partners to help them close the deal. Another colleague of mine felt that having the principals participate in a give-back project like building a house for Habitat for Humanity could provide that bonding experience. Florence and I were already talking and praying about the possibility of starting a new affiliate for Habitat for Humanity in DuPage County, Illinois, and had agreed that building a house for Habitat would be a great opportunity for us to become more familiar with the organization.

In early October 1994, we returned from our honeymoon in Hawaii. We'd enjoyed two weeks of gorgeous scenery, impressive snorkeling, and delicious meals, and we were emotionally and spiritually renewed and ready to move on. As we were talking about the possible sale of RJN Group, Florence told me that she thought the best place for the RJN principals to experience new trust would be by living together as a team for a week, building a house in the place where Habitat for Humanity was born—Americus, Georgia. What a concept! Could we really make it happen?

So we began to consider the trip to Americus, Georgia, even if we had to go without the principals. Florence said it would be another new experience for her, just as our honeymoon had been. Of course it probably wouldn't be with the same comfort and style (that would turn out to be an understatement!) but she assured me that she would take this part of our journey together. I told her that I appreciated her trust in me, and together we decided to undertake the challenge of presenting the idea of a corporate trip to Americus to the RJN principals.

At first glance, the idea was far-fetched. I was going to ask all eight of the principals at RJN Group to leave their homes, their families, their work, and their routines for an entire week. Instead they'd fly to a remote place they'd never heard of in southwest Georgia and build a house for a family they never met.

Why do it? How could I convince them (as well as their spouses) to set aside their everyday lives for an entire week? While the company would pick up the cost of the trip, including airfare, car rental, and the expense of staying in Americus, the real cost was having to be away from their families and routines—not to mention the physical and emotional demands of working as manual laborers for eight hours a day. I hoped though that the primary purpose of the trip, to bond as a group and develop the respect and trust necessary for a possible buy-out, would convince them.

Meanwhile, Florence and I learned everything we could about Habitat for Humanity and how a new affiliate in DuPage County might work. My company's home base and corporate office were located in Wheaton, Illinois, the county seat of DuPage County. I had lived in the county for thirty years, and my roots were deep. Despite the fact that there were ten other Habitat affiliates throughout the Chicago area, no one had ever successfully launched one in our county. A large part of the reason, we knew, was the perception that there was no need for Habitat in DuPage County. It is one of the country's wealthiest counties; at that time, the median family income was almost $55,000. Close to 40 percent of its adult residents have college degrees, and 74 percent of residents are homeowners.

In such a predominantly middle- to upper-class area, it was (and is) easy to overlook the 25,000 families living in substandard apartment complexes. We believed that a local Habitat affiliate could help change that. While Florence and I initially kept our Habitat plans to ourselves, we hoped that the experience of going to Americus would not only help the principals bond but would give us hands-on experience working for Habitat that we could use to help launch a local affiliate.

After discussing how to bring it up with Florence, I first approached Al in September 1994, about having the principals share in a weeklong retreat at Habitat. He was surprised at first. "But we don't know anything about Habitat!" he said, but he promised to keep an open mind. I wasn't going to give up. In the late 80s, I'd self-published a 5 x 5 inch book of quotations titled *We'll Find a Way* that was based on how RJN Group had tackled difficult problems presented by our engineering clients—and solved them more efficiently and cost-effectively than our competitors. "We'll Find a Way" become RJN's slogan in the industry, and we had three-inch buttons with the slogan that we wore at trade shows and conventions.

We'll find a way, I told Florence. And we would. We scheduled a meeting with the rest of the principals where I broached the idea of taking a trip to Americus, Georgia, to build a home for Habitat. I explained that Florence and I thought it would enhance their relationships and help facilitate the buyout.

The principals' initial response was not what I had hoped for. They were, in a word, dumbfounded, exchanging glances around the table. Their reactions were similar to Al's—why Habitat? Why spend an entire week building a house together? What was the point? I explained again that I believed that such an experience would help them develop the kind of relationship and trust that would enable them not only to acquire the company but to run it successfully thereafter. I could see, however, that they were not convinced. I knew I had more work to do to convince them that the trip wasn't just a crazy idea. I had to convince them that it would be worth their time and expense—but how?

When I called Habitat for Humanity International headquarters in Americus to ask about arrangements for such a trip, the staffers were surprised. While they had a program for college students (designed as an alternative to a typical college spring break), Habitat had never had a corporate team spend a week in Americus. The staff person I spoke with explained that the college spring break program allowed a group of college students to come to Americus, live in a neighborhood house for a week, build a new home at a Habitat worksite, and return to school enriched and "bonded" for the experience. That was the word I was listening for—bonded. I asked Habitat International to send me videos and materials that I could present to the principals.

About a month later, at an RJN Group business meeting, Florence and I gave another presentation about why the principals should accompany us to Americus for one week to build a house. Both Florence and I spoke about what we hoped to gain as individuals, and what we hoped the rest of the principals would experience as well. I remember Florence's excitement about the trip; she made the modest living conditions we'd have sound like an adventure.

While I wanted to insist that the principals take the trip, Florence convinced me not to make the trip mandatory. She wanted the principals themselves to agree that benefits to be gained would outweigh the unknowns and physical and emotional costs. Still, it was not an easy sell. Some said it would be too much of a disruption in both their business and personal lives. Some were under the impression it would be a religious experience designed to convert people or alter their beliefs, and two refused to go.

A few days later, however, six out of eight of the principals agreed to make the trip. Two of them brought their spouses, and two of my corporate administrators also joined the group. Our group included:

- Al Hollenbeck, who had been with RJN for seventeen years, working with me in the Wheaton office. He was vice-president and heir apparent to becoming managing partner, and one of my most trusted coworkers. Thin, quiet, and thoughtful, he is nonetheless a good leader, and I believed he was the right person to take over the company when I left. His wife, Karen, supported him going but could not make the trip.
- Scott Rebman, our resident information technology expert who managed the national computer services division from our Wheaton office; he had been with the company for five years but didn't spend a lot of time working with the other principals. Scott is a natural jokester, extroverted, and able to make just about anyone laugh. His wife Carolyn was unable to take time off from work to attend.
- Steve Maney, a civil engineer who was in charge of engineering services in the Wheaton office, and who had worked for RJN for fifteen years. He's a "typical" engineer in that he's somewhat reserved and introverted, but very good at his job.
- Hugh Kelso, the civil engineer in charge of the Dallas branch office. Although he had worked for RJN for ten

years, he didn't have close working relationships with other principals because he worked in a branch office instead of Wheaton. He's a good leader, though, and considered by all of us to be a strong "team player."

- Rich Zeimba, the civil engineer in charge of the Indianapolis office, who had been with RJN for more than ten years. Robust and hard-working, he's quick to pitch in when anyone needs a hand. His wife, Cheryl, accompanied him.

- Scott Paeth, an energetic, motivated civil engineer working in the Wheaton office who had been with the company for five years. At the time, he was the youngest of the group, and slightly overwhelmed by the prospect of the trip. His wife, Janet, came along as well.

- Susan Karcher and Angie Perri, two of my long-time dedicated office administrators, rounded out our group. I had asked Susan and Angie to join us for three reasons. First, I wanted them to bond with the potential new owners of the company. I also wanted them to gain a greater understanding of Habitat for Humanity in case I could talk Al into "loaning" them to us to help set up the new affiliate. Finally, I wanted them to enjoy some time away from the office.

Florence and I knew that our living quarters in Americus would be shared with "house parents." The "Amigo House," as it was called, could accommodate as many as twelve people. However, it only had two bedrooms and two baths! Each bedroom held six bunk beds, and we worried about how we'd divide the men and women up. The final signup consisted of seven men and five women . . . almost perfect for our plush two-bedroom accommodations.

People would be flying into Atlanta from several locations around the country and then make the three-hour drive to Americus. Florence and I had decided to arrive a few days ahead of time to learn more about Habitat. We met Millard and Linda Fuller, the founders of Habitat for Humanity International. Usually Habitat volunteers don't get this opportunity, but our RJN Foundation was a "Master Builder Donor" for their new headquarters that were being renovated a few blocks away from their existing offices. Millard and Linda also wanted to meet us as we had brought the first corporate team to build a home in Americus.

I was impressed with Millard's energy and enthusiasm. A tall, lanky man with glasses and an intense way about him, he peppered his speech with stories about the Habitat homeowners and the difference their new homes had made in their lives. One of his favorite sayings was "Oyée!", an African phrase which means "Praise God." I quickly learned that Millard was a consummate salesman—he'd been a successful lawyer and entrepreneur before he and Linda founded Habitat. He never took "no" for an answer and could quickly disarm any objections or doubts you might express with inspiring words.

On a warm Sunday in late October, six RJN Group executives, two of their wives, and two corporate administrators flew into Atlanta, rendezvoused at the airport, rented two vans, and drove caravan-style to Americus. On the way, Al remarked, "Be prepared. This is not going to be a Holiday Inn. We are in for a unique experience." How right he was.

At Amigo House, Florence and I were waiting for the principals, and getting to know our "house parents," Earl and Suzanne. The retired couple hailed from Indiana near the town of Spencer, where Florence's dad had grown up. Florence had spent time at her grandfather's farm as a little girl, and was delighted to reminisce with them about Spencer, including the covered bridge over the White River a few miles north of town. She told me later that it was like talking with her grandparents again.

Our Amigo House was an old frame house of about 1,000 square feet that included two bedrooms and two baths for visitors, plus a small living room, kitchen, and back porch. Though small, Earl and Suzanne kept the house spotless. Awaiting the RJN principals, I prayed that our week at Amigo House would be an experience to remember. When they drove up, we directed them to the makeshift parking area in the backyard, and welcomed them into a large screened-in back porch.

That first night, we were getting ready to drive to a local restaurant for pizza when our house parents called a group meeting on the back porch, which offered protection against the bugs buzzing around outside. Earl and Suzanne welcomed us and told us what to expect for the week. In the morning, we'd have a quick breakfast of cereal or something similar—no eggs, bacon, pancakes, or waffles. There also wouldn't be time for morning showers. After hammering nails all day in the hot sun, the twelve of us would have to figure out how we were going to get by with only two showers. This was one of the first tests of our organizational skills. However, the twelve of us resolved the challenge by returning in shifts at the end of each day.

Once indoors, most of the principals appeared a bit disturbed by the multitude of bunk beds in each bedroom and the obvious intimacy we'd all be experiencing. We also had to squeeze in a seventh bed in the all-male bedroom. But most smiled and shrugged. Florence heard several of the men joking about the sleeping quarters, saying the tight space reminded them of their college days. While all had been out of college for several years (or more), I appreciated their positive attitude. I hoped it was a sign of the week to come.

Everyone claimed his or her space, tossing their possessions on their chosen bunks. I watched Florence for a moment as she made up her bunk bed in the "girls' dorm." We had just returned from our honeymoon, and here we were about to sleep in separate bedrooms—for an entire week. I caught her eye, and winked with a small smile. I would miss her more than she realized. I hoped she could read my thoughts.

I knew she did when she winked back with a smile, as if to say, "It's okay." I wondered how many other newlywed couples would be willing to undertake this adventure so early in their marriage—and I was grateful that Florence was willing to do it with me.

The first night was the toughest. While it was October, the weather was hot and humid, something out of a Tennessee Williams novel. There was no air conditioning and no breeze, and most of us didn't sleep well that night. Before we fell asleep, several of us joked about who snored, and who claimed they didn't, and what we might do to those who kept us up. Finally, I fell asleep, wondering what the next day would bring.

The first morning, some of our group were surprised that we were all expected to attend services at the Habitat International headquarters building each morning. A Habitat volunteer opened the service with announcements, followed by several personal testimonies from speakers who talked about what it had meant to them to visit or work for Habitat. The thirty-minute service was a moving experience for me, but I wasn't sure how the other principals might react. Some felt like Habitat was trying to "convert" them.

We finished with a brief prayer for our safety as we worked, and departed for the tool shed to get our assigned tools and tool belts—our individual badges of honor. My tool belt was made of sturdy, scarred leather, with a groove worn into the notch where my hammer would hang. It felt heavy as I strapped it around my waist, but I appreciated the concrete evidence of what we were there to achieve. Then we drove as a group to the site where we would help build a new house, following our crew leader, Joe, to the building site about two miles away.

At the building site, we were shocked to see that there was no shell, no frame, nothing . . . except an empty concrete slab. The Habitat crew manager, Joe, didn't waste any time putting us to work—he couldn't afford to. Blond-haired, with a mustache and beard, thirty-year-old Joe was a full-time employee of Habitat, and as crew manager, he was in charge of building several houses simultaneously. As a result, he expected us to pay attention, learn what we needed to do, and to do it without having to stand over our shoulders. I glanced at some of the other principals, wondering if they were thinking what I was thinking—"I hope I don't let this guy down!"

Over time, we learned that he was not the "slave driver" that he first appeared to be, but a thoughtful and understanding teacher. For example, two of the principals, Scott and Steve, had never been particularly handy with tools. Both were surprised (and a little nervous) when Joe decided they should learn to use the circular saw to cut wood for the frame of the house. And so were the rest of us! Al, Hugh, and I took one look at Scott and Steve's early attempts and quickly moved to the roof to "give them some space."

After some trial and error, though, Steve learned how to hold the plywood boards steady as Scott powered up the saw, buzzing a straight line from one end to the other. One afternoon when Joe came to check their work, he nodded in approval. "Humph," he said, examining their stack of boards. "There's hope for you. Good progress today." I saw them catch each other's eye and grin. Over the week they developed a closer friendship.

Joe worked patiently with the rest of us on skills as basic as nailing. We slowly improved as we watched, learned, and hammered some nails straight and others crooked. Joe would come over to inspect our work, and then make us remove any crooked nails. After that occurred a few times, most of us self-corrected our hammering techniques. Eventually, Joe did not have to come back and say, "Good try. But they went in crooked—and here's how you make sure they go in straight." Crooked was just not acceptable.

The men and women worked together to construct and raise the wall frames. The roof trusses arrived on site already assembled, but had to be manually hoisted up to the roof one at a time. It was like a traditional Amish barn-raising—everyone on the ground helped lift the roof trusses to Hugh, Al, and me, who were balancing on top of the wood beams. Then the three of us nailed the roof plywood while others nailed the plywood to the exterior walls.

Over the coming days, we posed for pictures through the bare window frames that would soon be filled with glass windows. Several days that week, one of the children who would live in the house came by to help out. (We'd meet his mother, who worked full-time, on Saturday when she came to work on the house.) About twelve years old, he was reserved, hanging back to watch us at first. Then he began retrieving tools or other things we needed for our work. He told us he lived with his mother and younger brother, and I often saw him standing in the interior of the unfinished rooms. I thought he might be imagining what it would be like to live here in his own house, and to have his own bedroom.

The emotional rewards of giving back by those who had a lot, to those who had a little, became more evident each day.

Florence and I could see the changes taking place in the hearts and minds of the RJN people. On several occasions, several of us went to visit other Habitat homes and were struck by the pride their owners took in them. Houses often had decorative shutters, flower boxes, and colorful banners fluttering in the breeze. The yards were small but well-kept, and over and over we heard people talking about the difference Habitat had made for them and for their families. "If it weren't for Habitat," we heard more than once, "our family wouldn't be living together today."

I could see the principals developing trust and confidence in each other and I was starting to believe that this trip would have the results I'd hoped for. Scott said to me mid-week, "It's being in this environment. Only here would we get to know each other the way we are." (This was in the days before everyone carried a cell phone or BlackBerry®—that kind of bonding would be more difficult today when thanks to ubiquitous technology, everyone is always "wired" to the rest of the world.)

But we didn't spend all of our time working. In the evenings, we sat around playing board games and charades. We laughed and talked and grew closer in a way I had never expected. We were becoming more than coworkers and spouses. We were becoming partners and friends.

Take Hugh, a principal from the Dallas office. In addition to being more geographically isolated from the other offices, the Dallas office was the newest RJN Group office. Working with other principals helped Hugh get to know them, and to trust them with more than his career future. As we built wall frames, Hugh, Al, and I had to trust each other as we were raising the roof trusses as a team. That experience required each of us to depend on the other for our physical safety.

I saw Hugh, the only principal from the South, becoming comfortable with the rest of our group. At lunch break, Hugh would walk us over to a roadside stand and exclaim in his southern drawl, "Now, let me show you what I grew up with— balled peanuts." As we sampled the soft, salty treat, we finally figured out that the "balled" peanuts were actually "boiled."

During all those working days, none of us amateur house builders ever got hurt. We began to learn that if you can trust your business partner to cover your back and look out for you, then you could share your skill, strength, and support with him as well. The group also felt comfortable teasing Florence and me, ribbing us about being newlyweds who were forced to sleep not only in separate beds, but separate bedrooms as well!

After a few nights, Florence and I became concerned with the poor condition of everyone's bed pillows. After being used by hundreds of volunteers, they were flat, deflated, and offered little neck support. To help everyone sleep more comfortably, we drove to the local department store and brought back twelve new pillows.

We were shocked when we returned. Everyone had disappeared. Even their cars were gone! Had they deserted us after all? When we entered the house, a little concerned, we were soon greeted by "surprise!" as they all reappeared, laughing at pulling off their joke. After some good laughs, it was our turn to surprise them with their new pillows, which went a long way to making their beds more comfortable.

After that first stifling night, the weather cooled off, and we had warm, sunny days and cooler nights. While my back and arms were sore from the unaccustomed labor, I didn't hear any complaints from anyone about the physical demands of the week. But I was still surprised when Al approached me one morning before we left for the job site and said all of the principals had decided to not only attend the morning service on their last day, but would like to conduct it. I called the Habitat office to ask about Al's request. The staff said as far as they could remember, they never had a company conduct or host the morning services but that they would be pleased and honored.

On that last Friday morning, the sun was shining, and the weather was warm. After eating our usual quick breakfast and strapping on our tool belts, the twelve of us walked together the two blocks to headquarters.

During the service, the RJN principals took the podium to tell those present how the week had affected them and what it had meant to their lives. They talked about taking risks, and how the experience had made them more grateful for what they had in their own lives, whether it was a college education or family financial support they could rely on. I knew they had seen firsthand that Habitat homeowners weren't "unmotivated" or "lazy" but rather unlucky—the circumstances of their lives, often out of their control, had placed them in situations that were hard to escape from. I saw and heard true empathy from my fellow RJN staff and was truly moved.

They also mentioned how they'd come to trust one another with their personal safety at the work site. Whenever two of us were nailing shingles on the roof, we knew that if you slipped, your partner would catch you. That trust was simply there. Earlier in our relationship, Florence had told me about the time she had to replace roof shingles on her house. While some friends had volunteered to reroof her home, she soon discovered she had to be the "cheerleader" and get them started every day, and sometimes even stay up on the roof with them to keep them working. It wasn't a good experience for her and she was determined never again to climb up on a roof and shingle . . . never.

One morning while some of us were shingling, Florence and several others were "walking the site" to pick up nails and debris that had accumulated during the day. Out of nowhere,

Joe came up to Florence and said in a very strong voice, "We need help up on the roof. Do you think you can shingle for a while?"

Joe had not spoken directly to Florence all week. Her first thought was to scream, "NO!" But she waited three seconds and decided this must not be just a coincidence. She joined the rest of us on the roof, and sat side by side nailing away.

That's why one of my favorite pictures of the two of us shows Florence and me on the roof of the house we built in Americus, nailing shingles. I remember what she said afterwards—that some old emotional wounds had been healed by shingling with me, and trusting that I wouldn't let her fall. "Until we get this roof done," she said, "I'm going to let myself just laugh—and keep on nailing."

It wasn't until that last service, though, that Al told us that his mother had been hospitalized just before he left his home in Wheaton for Americus. He was really torn about coming to Americus, but decided to make the trip. Each day while Al was in Americus working for Habitat, his mother had steadily improved. Al inspired everyone with his message of faith and humility as he spoke to us about his own fears—his fear that he may have left his mother's side when she needed him and his fear that he would not be an effective leader for the new company. With words and warm smiles, the other principals assured him they had confidence in his abilities. There was not a dry eye in the room.

Listening to the principals, I thought they were beginning to imagine the company being run differently than it had with me as the boss. They were envisioning working together as a cohesive group as opposed to having one majority owner. Time would tell, but I thought they had begun laying the foundation that they would need.

The evening before we were to leave Americus, we returned to our job site and took photos of the house we'd built. The walls were straight and tall and the roof was finished; in three or four weeks, it would be completed and ready to move into. We took a marker and wrote our signatures and best wishes for God's blessings on all who entered the house on the inside of the plywood. While it would be covered by the drywall which other volunteers would hang, our names and our work would always be a part of the house. The woman who would live in the house was there that evening with both of her sons, and we had a chance to say tearful, yet joyful good-byes.

The next morning the principals left Americus and drove to Atlanta to catch their flights home. I knew they were thinking about their decision of a lifetime . . . to buy or not to buy the engineering firm.

And me? I was exhausted, as was Florence. We stayed in Americus to say good-bye to Earl and Suzanne. We checked into a local motel and basked in the comfort of a long hot shower, a king-sized bed . . . and each other.

Millard Fuller had suggested that before we left Americus, we visit Plains, Georgia, home of former President Jimmy Carter. On Sunday morning, we listened to him lead the Bible study at the Maranatha Baptist Church. It was an amazing experience to see the former president of our country talking about his personal faith, and sharing a prayer with him. Afterwards we were able to speak with him briefly, but I did not know at the time that I would meet and talk again with President Carter in the future—about a strange hitchhiker I'd met.

Millard had told us earlier how perseverance came to be a key to Habitat's success. Millard and Linda Fuller started Habitat in 1976, and while growth was steady, Millard knew that getting President Carter's endorsement and involvement could result in tremendous growth. After President Carter gave his endorsement to Habitat in 1986, he and his wife Rosalynn worked on Habitat sites throughout the world, and the organization grew exponentially. While it took ten years of continual persuasion by Millard to get former President Carter involved (remember, he never took "no" as an answer), today he and Rosalynn set aside one week each year for the Habitat for Humanity International "Jimmy Carter Blitz Build." The rest of the year, their time is devoted to the Carter Center.

We stayed a few more days in Americus to talk with Millard and learn more about the mechanics of setting up an affiliate for Habitat for Humanity in DuPage County. Florence and I had big plans and big dreams, but now we needed to actually put them into action. DuPage County is located west of Chicago and encompasses thirty-four municipalities, and about one million people. It would be a major undertaking. One of the first things I did when we returned to Wheaton was network with many old friends—some of them went as far back as my civil rights days in the 60s—and with other DuPage County civic and business leaders.

I invited these friends and community leaders to attend the first formation meeting of DuPage Habitat for Humanity at the former RJN headquarters. RJN had grown out of its original building in 1980, moving across the street to much larger quarters. The newly emptied space would be perfect headquarters for the new affiliate of Habitat in DuPage County. A total of seventeen of them agreed to serve on our new board of directors.

Upon returning to Wheaton, I also waited to hear from the RJN principals. While they couldn't stop talking about the trip, I wasn't receiving any feedback about a consensus to buy or not to buy. So I continued to wait.

The bank was ready, the accountant was ready, the lawyers were ready, and the ESOP was ready. Most of the employees were ready, but it was now up to the principals. Were they ready? They still needed to sign the agreements and the necessary personal guarantees.

About thirty days had passed when Al walked into my office. "Dick, I want you to know that we are ready to go," he said with a smile. "We are going to do it. We are going to buy the company!"

Scott would later take me aside and tell me that taking the trip to Americus had been a major factor in their decision. The confidence and trust the principals had developed in each other enabled them to take the leap of faith to actually buy the company. My belief, that when the principals interacted in that environment they would gain the confidence to buy the company, had been validated. "Dick, I'm convinced that it may not have happened if we didn't have the Habitat experience before buying the firm," Scott told me. "We learned to partner together and that the company could be passed on to new leadership."

In the meantime, I vacated my office in RJN's new, larger headquarters and moved back to my original office in the old RJN building which would become the new offices for the RJN Foundation as well as for Habitat. Due to selling RJN Group, Florence and I could now fund the RJN Foundation, and we created a five-person board of directors—Al, Scott, Chuck, Florence, and me.

It's not a surprise that after all this, Florence and I were now ready for a planned vacation to one of our favorite places, the Turks and Caicos Islands in the Caribbean. We would be heading to the town of Providenciales.

When we were in Americus, we had learned about Habitat's "Vacation with a Purpose" program. We remembered that there might be a group going to the Dominican Republic in January to build in that Third World country. We were surprised to discover that the trip to the Dominican Republic for Habitat for Humanity International was scheduled two weeks before our already scheduled trip to Turks and Caicos. Coincidence or divine intervention? Florence and I prayed about it, and decided to take both trips, back to back.

We arranged to rendezvous in Miami with a church group coming from Fort Worth, Texas for its "Vacation with a Purpose." Together we would continue on our give-back adventure to a place called Barahona, located on the southwest coast of the Dominican Republic, fifty miles east of the border with Haiti.

Passports ready, shots taken, Imodium in hand, gifts for the folks we would visit, reading materials that would prepare us for what we thought we were about to experience, we boarded the plane—looking forward to the next part of our extraordinary journey.

Chapter Three

IF YOU HAVE TWO GLOVES, GIVE ONE TO ANOTHER

AFTER THE HOLIDAYS, FLORENCE and I flew to the Dominican Republic for our month-long trip. The first part would be our "Vacation with a Purpose," traveling as part of a team to the town of Barahona to help build Habitat homes in one of the poorest parts of this Third World country. (Habitat's Vacation with a Purpose program lets participants pay their own way and then make a donation to the foreign Habitat affiliate they are visiting.) The second part would be a true vacation. After our work for Habitat, we planned to vacation in the Turks and Caicos Islands, just north of the Dominican Republic, and get some much-needed rest and relaxation. At least that was the plan.

We met our companions for this adventure at the Miami Airport before we flew to the D.R. Sue, Sandy, John, Beth, and Joe were all members of a church in Fort Worth, Texas, and quickly made us feel like part of their group. Joe was an internist, about thirty, married to Beth; John was a tall, dark-haired athletic guy in his late twenties, and Sandy was about forty, with dark hair. Sue, a forty-something physical therapist, was blond and athletic, and a natural leader. Later, at the Santo

Domingo Airport, we met Joan and Herron, another couple from Texas. Both in their mid-fifties, Herron was a pediatrician and Joan was a teacher.

Arriving in Santo Domingo, we were greeted by Chris and Steve, the couple that operated the Habitat affiliate in Barahona. They were both in their late twenties, bilingual, and strikingly attractive with charismatic personalities. We immediately liked them. Several years prior, they had decided to leave promising journalism careers at the *Chicago Tribune* to run the Habitat affiliate in Barahona. Chris' parents were missionaries and she had always wanted to do something similar. After they were married a few years and before starting a family, Steve told Chris he wanted to give her a special gift. He would agree to quit his job and go with her to Barahona for three years to fulfill her dream. Then they would return to Chicago and settle down. Both Florence and I were impressed with their relentless energy and enthusiasm. (Years later, we learned that Chris and Steve had had two children—and were still working for Habitat in Barahona! So "three years" turned into much longer.)

In Santo Domingo, we experienced what locals took for granted—dozens of armed military personnel patrolling the streets and sidewalks. While we never were stopped by them, their presence made us nervous. We kept our passports with us at all times. The town was a mix of older buildings with some new ones, and the people were generally shorter and thinner than us. The cars were different, too—vehicles tended to be older and smaller than what you'd see in the States, and once we traveled out of town, almost all of the cars were small, "beater" models.

Despite the military presence, we felt comfortable there; people were generally friendly toward us. We toured a historic fort, old churches, and markets where we saw handmade embroidered clothing for sale. We talked and joked with many of the street vendors since several in our group spoke fluent Spanish. That evening we all went to the hotel restaurant for dinner and experienced a real treat. We were entertained by a local band and learned how to salsa dance.

After spending two days touring Santo Domingo, we headed for Barahona, a three-hour bus ride away. The bus windows were wide open as the air conditioning was not working—if it had ever worked. We did have an "experienced" driver who apparently never felt the need to slow down. His bravery made for a terrifying ride on a narrow, bumpy two-lane highway.

The road had two lanes with a four-foot paved shoulder on each side. If someone wanted to pass another vehicle, the vehicle in front would move onto the shoulder, leaving half the lane open, and the oncoming traffic would do the same— leaving just enough room for the passing vehicle to travel down the middle of the road, turning it into a three-lane highway! It was a harrowing experience for anyone not used to these creative driving maneuvers—like us.

As we drove further away from the capital, we saw alarming poverty. While there were countless roofless concrete block shells, few were actually finished. Chris and Steve told us that those working for reelection of the existing government received concrete blocks to finish their homes. Away from the capital, there were fewer voters, and fewer concrete blocks, resulting in fewer finished homes. Most houses had flimsy metal roofs, many of which would be blown away with the next hurricane.

We saw women washing clothes in river creeks, sweeping out floors and porches onto the roads, and grocery shopping. Men congregated in groups along the roads, or at local bars, and children in school uniforms walked along the road with books under their arms. We were sad to learn that the children of the poorest families were not allowed to attend school because their parents could not afford to purchase school uniforms. Younger kids played games in the streets, shouting and laughing; little boys were often naked but little girls usually had well-worn cotton dresses on.

As we continued, I thought the only thing missing from this bus ride were chickens on the bus roof, like in the movie *Romancing the Stone*. We made a few stops, both for lunch and to pick up a few new passengers. The roadside café was a regular stop on the bus route, and its expansive front was completely open without windows or doors. The dinette tables were rather drab metal and gray Formica but the building itself was painted bright yellow with red trim, and colorful posters and textiles adorned the walls. My lunch of chicken burritos and rice was quite delicious. About halfway into the trip, military personnel stopped the bus. Guns drawn and faces impassive, four soldiers entered the bus, walking up and down the aisle, carefully eyeballing each of us. If they were looking for someone in particular, they did not find him, and we were allowed to continue.

When we finally arrived in Barahona, shaken but relieved, we were encouraged by the sight of the town. The city center area had paved streets with curbs, and a sprawling green park surrounding a plaza with a beautiful wooden gazebo for band concerts and dancing. It appeared to be a somewhat thriving urban setting with a population of about 20,000 people. As our bus drove away from the center of town, however, we found the roads unpaved and full not only of holes, but craters.

Houses were very small by our standards, measuring about 600 square feet. The poorest lived in frame homes with dirt floors and tin roofs. The more substantial homes were constructed of concrete block but still had tin roofs. The Barahona Habitat affiliate constructed its homes out of cinder block walls on cement slabs with poured cement roofs. Most of our group would stay in completed Habitat homes.

The bus dropped our group off, one couple at a time, at their temporary living quarters until only two couples were left, Florence and me along with Beth and Joe. We reached a modest blue frame house next to a small cement block building; Beth and Joe would be staying at the home of Don Gabriel and Donna Esmeralda. Don Gabriel was the executive director of the Barahona Habitat Affiliate. A native of Barahona, he had been working for Habitat for ten years.

Don Gabriel told us that plans for us to stay with another family had fallen through and the only place available was the small concrete block Habitat office next to Don Gabriel's home. Smaller than a single-wide trailer, it included a small office in front and a room of similar size in the back that was crammed with a double bed, a table for our suitcases (to keep them off of the damp cement floor), another small table, and a small fan that sometimes worked.

While our living quarters were snug, we were grateful to be next door and be able to share meals with Don Gabriel, his wife, and ten children, along with Beth and Joe. We had already discovered that we had intermittent electricity only a few hours a day, no running water, and no indoor bathroom. After dinner, we retired to our "bedroom" next door and unpacked. Our bed had a sagging middle, which made for easy cuddling but difficult sleeping. We lay next to each other whispering and wondering what we got ourselves into. We knew that we were here to learn more about God's plan for us, but what was that plan? We prayed together, asking for strength, guidance, and rest. After a wearying day, we both drifted off to sleep.

After a quick breakfast of scrambled eggs, fried plantains, and fruit, we were immediately put to work. We hand-mixed concrete and took part in a "bucket brigade" at one of the house sites. That first day, we helped pour footings for one of the thirty houses in various stages of construction. Steve and Chris had told us that Habitat builds thirty houses at a time, in three tiers of ten each. First they build ten slab floors. Then they build the walls of ten houses. Then they roof all ten houses. That way all ten houses get finished at the same time, and then they start another batch of homes.

The Habitat philosophy is based on "sweat equity," where the homeowner is required to invest several hundred hours on the construction of his or her own house. But these hours are too few to build and finish a house. Back in the States there would be plenty of volunteers to swing a hammer, and they would make up the difference in the labor and time needed.

In a Third World area such as Barahona, however, there are few volunteers. When everyone is poor, few can give back. Most people are simply trying to survive and make enough money working mostly at service jobs and any odd job they can get. With ten houses under construction at any given time, the prospective owners didn't just put time in on their own homes; they all helped each other. The ones who helped the most got their homes finished first, and the ones who helped less saw "their" homes fall back toward the end of the line. It was a system that seemed to be working.

At the job site the first day, we were warmly welcomed as "gringos" or the "Norte Americanos" from the States. The people there were appreciative of our contribution and to the physical work required. They were working for a payoff—their own homes—and were surprised that anyone would simply volunteer because they wanted to. They treated us with respect, and I realized that we had an opportunity to represent the United States. We wanted the Dominicans to know Americans as a peace-loving, friendly, and respectful people. It became clear to me that we weren't there just on a house-building mission but on a peace-making mission as well. Within a few days, we would be affectionately referred to as "amigos," or friends.

As Florence and I continued to work together and alongside the other volunteers and locals, our own bond grew stronger. We'd thought that the conditions in Americus were less than ideal but that was four-star luxury compared to how we were living now! After returning home from the work site the first day, we explored our backyard bathroom, or baño. A little bit larger than an outhouse, our baño was a tiny cement block building with two chambers. One chamber had a regular toilet with no running water; the other side had a fifty-five-gallon drum filled with water. After using the toilet, you filled a plastic bucket with water from the large drum and flushed it manually.

The water in the drum was fairly clean but cold. A local family filled the drum periodically, using a small hose that snaked through the backyards from the water plant. If the water plant in town was operating, the hose would have water. If not, no water. On this day, the drum had been recently filled, so the water was very cold. On the other hand, we were both sweaty and tired, and the temperature hovered in the 90s.

"What do you think, Florence? Shall we shower?" I looked at her and grinned.

"Let's do it." Her words weren't cautious, but her tone was. We shed our clothes together, lathered up, and proceeded to pour cold water from the bucket over each other until the soap was gone, bellowing out a chorus of "'O sole mio" to dull the shocking cold. The neighbors probably thought we were *locos*—nuts!

Because wood and nails are very expensive in the D.R., the lumber used to form the roofs was one of the most expensive commodities on the island. One day all Florence and I did was remove nails from the old wooden forms so they could be used over and over again. Several times when a roof was formed and ready to be poured the next day, we discovered in the morning that the wood had disappeared—taken by someone who needed it more than we did.

In Barahona, the major difference between a Habitat house and a local house was the roof material. A Habitat house has a concrete roof, poured manually one bucket at a time. While it is much more stable than a metal roof, pouring it is a time-consuming, arduous task. About six of us would stand in a circle, mixing sand, cement, and water on the dirt road near the house entrance and fill heavy-duty two-gallon plastic buckets. The buckets would then be passed up to the people on the roof pouring the concrete one bucket at a time.

The process was slow, in part due to the fact that we only had a small number of buckets to work with. I realized if we had more buckets, we could speed up the process. In addition, Chris said if we could get a roof poured in the morning, we might be able to take a trip to the beach in the afternoon. I gave Chris two hundred dollars to go back into town and purchase ten new, heavy-duty buckets to carry the hand-mixed wet concrete up to the roof.

With more buckets available, we organized the concrete mixing group so we all took turns doing the heavy work of mixing the concrete. A brigade of individuals made up of us and local Habitat families on ladders passed half-filled concrete buckets, one-to-one, eventually handing them to the people on the roof. I was in charge of filling the buckets and getting them passed to the brigade.

The locals quickly named me their honorary "Jimmy Carter," because whenever I would inadvertently fill a bucket with too much concrete, I would have to yell out, "Grande, grande" ["large, large"] so they knew it was heavier than normal. They in turn would respond, "Jimmy Carter, Jimmy Carter." We might have had a language barrier, but we laughed and joked together through this shared experience.

After the men on the roof poured the concrete, they tossed the empty buckets to the ground. I organized a group of neighborhood boys who would pick up the empty buckets and bring them back to us so we could fill them with more concrete. The boys were about ten or eleven, and enjoyed being a part of the process. Like many American boys, they were obsessed with baseball, but to the Dominican boys, baseball is more than a pastime. It can be a ticket out of poverty and into the world at large. The boys wanted to know where I came from and what baseball teams I followed, and I was surprised at how many players' names they knew. I told them I would give them each a major league baseball cap for helping us. They were elated and eager to help.

Florence and I also grew closer to our hosts, Don Gabriel and Esmeralda. We spent some evenings playing their favorite game of dominoes and although Florence and I never managed to win, in the last game, they let us come close. The score was 250 to 235. It wasn't about winning a game—it was about losing ourselves in new experiences and developing a deeper understanding of the common values we shared with the local families. We may have had more material possessions and money in the bank than our hosts, but we were the ones receiving love, care, and respect, to say nothing of the good cooking and hospitality, from our hosts.

Florence and I had brought twice as many suitcases as everyone else. Most of the group had come to stay for about ten days before returning home. As we were moving on to the Turks and Caicos Islands for the balance of the month, we had packed one set of suitcases for each trip. As the week progressed, however, we tapped into both suitcases, slowly giving away clothes and other items that we had brought.

Ella, the twenty-year-old daughter of Don Gabriel and Esmeralda, was a beautiful young woman with a shy smile and long, straight dark hair. She had noticed that if there was electric power, Florence would blow-dry her hair after showering and before dinner. One evening, Ella approached Florence and asked politely, "Could I please do your hair for you?"

"I would love that," said Florence with a smile. As Florence relaxed under Ella's careful touch, Ella told us that she wanted to start a hair salon out of her home. She admired the special round brush, comb, and blow dryer that Florence relied on every day—or at least every day the power worked. Florence had admitted that even in this environment, the ability to dry and style her hair made her feel more confident and pulled together. I was surprised when at the end of the trip, she left her blow dryer and styling accessories with Ella—on the eve of our own two-week vacation! I was impressed that Florence would do this knowing how vain she was about her hair. It gave me a new insight into Florence that touched me deeply. Florence wrote in her journal that day:

> I feel very proud of myself to know I can give away
> things that I "need." I used those things most every
> day and so it meant that I would have to just adjust,
> and that would be okay.

Thanks to our newly organized bucket brigade, we were able to finish roofs early in the afternoon on several days. This gave us time to board the "limo," or "gua gua," as the locals call it, and head to the beach. However, it was a limo in name only, as Florence noted in her journal:

> The transportation this time was a pickup truck
> with a metal cage around the top and a blue plastic
> cloth roof. About eight people rode inside and three
> or four rode on the top! We drove very fast and
> swayed back and forth—very scary! We did arrive
> safely at the beach, thank God.

There was no sand at the beach. Instead, the clear water of the Caribbean lapped up to large smooth pebbles. Fresh water flowed to the beach from the hills north of the beach; if you dug a hole on the beach, it filled with fresh water instead of salt water. This natural wonder turned out to be a welcome blessing for me as I had been dealing with an irritated bite on the front of my lower right leg for several days.

While I don't know what bit me, my guess was a spider—we saw spiders the size of ping-pong balls throughout Barahona. On one of our first nights there, Florence and I had just lay down in bed when we leaped up faster than I would have believed possible. We both saw it at the same time—a gigantic, black, hairy spider climbing the wall across from our bed. Neither of us wanted to go near it, let alone kill it! We hurried next door, telling Don Gabriel we had an emergency. When he came in, he laughed, casually removed his shoe, and smashed it in one blow. "Not to worry," he said. "It wasn't poisonous anyway."

I'd tried to clean the bite out with our small supply of bottled drinking water, but it hadn't improved. At the beach, I could see it had gotten worse, with a four-inch-long red streak emanating from the bite. Joe, an internist, examined my leg and promised to give me an antibiotic when we got back to the house. I was grateful there was a doctor with us!

In the meantime, I dug a hole on the beach and soaked my leg in the fresh water, cleaning out the bite with shampoo that we brought with us. It drained almost completely, and cleared up over the next few days. The rest of the day, we might have been on vacation. I wrote in my journal:

> This afternoon we hiked up to the waterfall, but about two-thirds of the way up the path it became too narrow. I was not comfortable with it, and then Florence slipped and turned her ankle. We decided to

go back and not to go all the way to the top. We came back down and stopped at one of the pools, washed up and then shampooed our hair in the river. It was quite refreshing and different, another first for us.

At night, the heat, humidity, and insects—not to mention our bed—made it difficult to sleep. That was the most challenging part of the trip—not just the work itself but the continual exhaustion we felt. People in Barahona didn't really have house pets, but there were always lots of animals freely roaming around. Dogs of all sizes slept all day in the heat of the sun and then foraged for food in the dark of the night. Dog packs would bark wildly during the night, fighting over scraps of food. After we finally did fall asleep, a rooster would wake us up at sunrise. At least we were never late for work at the building site in the morning.

That night, I prayed for restful sleep. As I lay next to Florence, I wrote in my journal:

> Dear God, please let me relax and sleep tonight. Keep the dogs quiet. Anything you can do, Lord, will help a lot. Florence and I took three Excedrin PMs tonight, and she is conked out next to me as I write this. This is sure a contrast from our last trip, which was to the South Seas Resort in Captiva, Florida. Things are very hard to describe. I do not know if this whole thing makes sense or not. Maybe by the end of the week we will have a better idea.

Florence and I had both brought an extra pair of leather work gloves from the States for ourselves, but each of us had given them to someone else who needed them. Mine had gone to one of the family homeowners who was helping me remove nails from ragged wooden forms. One afternoon,

Florence saw the woman she had given her spare pair to. While the woman was working at the building site, Florence noticed she was only wearing one glove. The woman working next to her, her friend, was wearing the other glove. We later talked about what we witnessed, and asked ourselves, "Is this a manifestation of Jesus' words when He said, 'If you have two coats, you will give one to another who has none.'?" I wrote in my journal that night:

> I think this was a very successful week in what we were able to accomplish on our peace-making mission. I believe that people will forever be aware of the goodwill and spirit of the Norte Americanos from the States. I know I will never forget so many of the people here who are just like an extended family. I understand what an old friend, Gene Boivin, talked to me about twenty-five years ago, a lot more clearly now.

Before we made the trip, the folks back in Americus had told us to bring baseball caps from the States for the young boys. Being both a Cubs and White Sox fan (rather a rare breed, I am told), I brought a dozen caps in my suitcase. The last day we were there, I handed them out to my young helpers. They smiled and positioned the caps on their heads, laughing as they experimented with the perfect angle. I've rarely seen someone appreciate any gift more.

(About twelve years since that day in Barahona, I was on my computer reviewing the Chicago White Sox roster. I was surprised to see that four of the White Sox starters were from the D.R.; one was twenty-two years old and listed his hometown as Barahona. Could he have been one of those smiling boys?)

On our last day at the job site, we finished one more roof and said good-bye, sharing hugs with both prospective homeowners and current homeowner workers at the house sites. In addition to taking group pictures at the work site, Florence and I also arranged for special pictures of Don Gabriel and his family. We promised that we would have the best photo enlarged, framed, and sent special delivery to Chris and Steve so they could bring the photo to Don Gabriel personally. Later, we received a card from Chris and Steve telling us how that family photo hangs proudly in Don Gabriel's living room for family and visitors to admire.

With joyous tears and unforgettable memories to last a lifetime, we boarded the bus for Santo Domingo. We arrived at the airport and said good-bye to our partners from Fort Worth. We had enjoyed their company and support and hope they felt the same way. Florence and I said our last farewell and got on the plane to fly back to Miami. We planned a one-night stay-over at the Miami airport hotel; we'd then fly out the next day to Turks and Caicos for a vacation of rest and relaxation.

The flight to Miami was more than memorable. We were flying on a DC-10 from Santo Domingo. Upon leveling off at our cruising altitude, we began to experience considerable turbulence and suddenly found ourselves engulfed in an incredible storm. We simultaneously saw and heard a lightning bolt right outside our window. Most of the passengers were from the Dominican Republic, and many of them immediately began praying in Spanish to themselves.

CAAARACK! Another streak of lightning shattered the murmured prayers and the lights went out. "Oh my God!" and "Ay dios mio!" rang through the cabin. Any attempt at remaining calm disappeared. Prayer books and rosaries emerged from everywhere as passengers prayed as loud as they could—in Spanish. Florence and I held each other tightly and prayed for our families. Would this be our last trip together? After what seemed like an eternity, we exited the storm. The captain, a slight tremble in his voice, came on the intercom. "I'm sorry, folks. No one ahead of us reported going through this weather front. We have been hit by lightning twice but have sustained no damage. We are now clear of this bad weather and should miraculously make it to Miami just fine." Florence and I hugged each other and gave thanks for what would lie ahead and for the additional time we were given to continue our extraordinary journey.

Upon landing safely in Miami, we discovered that same storm had turned the airport into a confused mass of humanity. We hurried to the desk of the airport hotel to see if we could get a room for that night. The desk clerk tried not to laugh and said that he was completely booked. I asked him to please look again, and he finally found a junior suite, the only remaining room in the hotel. We took it.

After gathering our bags, the bellhop led us to the fourteenth floor. Each suite on the floor was named after a Caribbean location. When we reached our room, we saw its name—"The Turks and Caicos Island Suite." We laughed out loud. What a coincidence! Upon entering the luxurious room, we felt that we had just received our reward for the past two weeks. A long, hot shower, a good American hamburger from room service, and simply being together that night prepared us for our trip to Turks and Caicos (what locals call "the Islands") the next day.

Florence and I had been to Turks once before and fallen in love with the place except for one thing. There were still pockets of poverty throughout the islands as well as a lack of affordable housing, especially in Providenciales, the largest city.

At the Providenciales airport, we went through customs, rented a car, and checked into our hotel to catch up on some rest. Then we set out to explore the island of "Provo," as the locals call it. We stumbled upon a residential neighborhood where some new modest, prefabricated homes were being built. The house pieces were made in Canada, then shipped and reassembled in Provo.

We introduced ourselves to the builder, a Canadian in his late forties, and told him about our recent Habitat building adventures. The houses he was building were designed to be affordable for the average working family—they were about 1,000 square feet, with walls made of cement panels. Houses sat on cinderblock footings, and each had a front porch with railings. As we discussed the need for affordable housing, he suggested that we meet with the powers-that-be in Providenciales as well as the prime minister and other officials on Grand Turk, a nearby island and the capital of Turks and Caicos. He thought the officials might be willing to bring Habitat to the Islands, and that we were the perfect people to pitch the idea.

The next day, Florence and I set out for the local administrative offices on Provo to discuss Habitat. The officials we met with liked the idea and helped arrange for us to fly to Grand Turk to meet with their prime minister. At the time, however, the Islands were in the middle of a heated election. One administrator admitted that we might not get the attention we needed due to the split in political views and that consensus might be difficult to achieve. But he added, "There is a substantial need for affordable housing on these Islands. The homes that the builder you met is building are only a fraction of the housing needed here in the Turks and Caicos Islands." As we grew excited about bringing Habitat here, we forgot all about our holiday plans. It was only later that Florence and I would say to each other, "Wasn't this part of the trip supposed to be our vacation?"

The weather, however, continued to be very windy, cutting back our planned beach time at the Ocean Club and snorkeling at Smith Reef. Instead we confirmed our meeting on Grand Turk with Prime Minister Conrad Higgs and other officials to talk about the possibility of having them start an affiliate of Habitat for Humanity in Turks and Caicos. Florence and I met several gracious officials on Grand Turk but they were not encouraging. According to them, many of the housing problems were centered on Haitian nationals who were in the Islands illegally.

Living conditions for poor people in Haiti are incredibly bad—the large cities contain slums with cardboard boxes for homes and no running water. In the Turks and Caicos, while there are poor people, there are no slums per se and more decent housing is available. Illegal immigrant Haitians will accept living in rental homes that are poorly maintained, simply because the homes are much better than what they would have had in Haiti. This, according to the officials, made it easier for unscrupulous landlords to continue to rent substandard housing.

In addition, Provo was beginning to become a "vacation home" destination, which meant that there might be fewer housing options for native Belongers, or Turks and Caicos nationals. All the organizations that might be able to help were quite small and had very limited staffs and budgets, so it was clear that the housing problem here was only going to get worse.

We returned to the hotel with a large list of letters to be written, people to contact, and other tasks to address when we got back to the States. That night I wrote in my diary:

> Yesterday was the highlight of this part of our trip
> as we flew to Grand Turk. In the morning, we got
> up early and took an 8:30 A.M. flight on Turks and
> Caicos Airways. It was on an old two-engine prop
> VHQ that seats eight passengers. It was awesome

to fly over the Caicos bank—hundreds of square miles of two feet deep water—until you get to the Turks and Caicos passage before Grand Turk. We were surprised to find an island where time was practically suspended. The character of the terrain was very different, the people are friendly, and everything is close, clean, and somewhat weather beaten from the salt water. Trees are not plentiful as they were stripped out years ago. It resulted in water shortages. There are no wells—only cisterns that collect water when it rains. Also, there are wild horses and donkeys on the island.

We spent the balance of our time together on Provo sunning, swimming, snorkeling, and enjoying delicious seafood meals—more like a "real" vacation. But the seeds that had been planted were already beginning to sprout. Both of us felt called to continue Habitat's work, as individuals and as a couple. The last journal entry I wrote on our way back to the States read:

> I think a lot about our future and our partnership, and how important it is to go ahead with God's plan for us. While in Turks, we had some time to think and rest and I was grateful for that. Yesterday, before we left, I was sick, but in the afternoon, I took a hot shower and felt many times better. How is it that our friends in Christ back in Barahona will go through their life and never experience a hot shower? For me, it is both confusing and profound.

Chapter Four

"NOT IN *MY* BACK YARD"

IT WAS LATE JANUARY 1995, and we had just returned home from our back-to-back trips to the Dominican Republic and the Turks and Caicos Islands. Before we'd left, Florence and I met with and received commitments from seventeen dedicated leaders in the business community to serve on the first board of Habitat for Humanity in DuPage County. We had attained "affiliate" status from Habitat International, and set up offices in the original RJN Group building. Our new blue and white glistening metal DuPage Habitat for Humanity sign was proudly displayed on the front of the building.

We held our first board meeting on February 1st. We welcomed the new board members, took group photos, signed the mission and purpose covenants required by Habitat for Humanity International, and officially launched the affiliate. We were committed not only to starting an affiliate that would provide an opportunity for volunteers and "hammer swingers" to give back to the community but that would also provide a way for local families to own their own homes. Our hope— as lofty as it was—was that Habitat would help parents and their children achieve their full potential by having a stable, comfortable home base.

We would ask for God's help in the process, and Habitat would be the vehicle that would act as a partner to nurture families. Many people were excited about having a Habitat affiliate in DuPage County. We had learned that there were about 25,000 families living in what the county officially considered to be substandard housing when compared to typical standard housing at that time. These apartments or rental homes might have malfunctioning kitchen stoves or refrigerators that landlords refused to repair; plumbing or roofs that leaked; inoperable windows and doors; insect and/or rodent infestations; and heating and air conditioning that didn't work—or a combination of the above. Despite some people's perceptions, there was no shortage of need—just a desperate lack of availability of affordable decent housing for these families. County officials knew that these families needed affordable housing; however, the public perception in this generally well-to-do place was that there was no need.

As members of the board discussed how to proceed, it didn't take us long to discover some differences of opinion. One major conflict was just how fast we should try to build. Should we borrow funds and purchase properties to build immediately or should we wait, raise the funds first, and then begin building?

Another concern of the board was that one of Habitat's purposes was to raise the public's consciousness about the plight of the families who lived in substandard housing. That discussion quickly became confrontational because of strong political, religious, and economic overtones. Florence and I and some of the other board members believed that simply building a house here and there wasn't sufficient to fulfill Habitat's mission. We needed to let people know about the problem, there in their own communities, of substandard housing and to inspire them to do something about it. Other board members weren't comfortable with the consciousness-raising aspect of Habitat and wanted to focus only on the house-building aspect.

Privately, Florence and I felt these overtones were closely related to one of Jesus' messages. He said, "For everyone to whom much is given, from him much will be required" (Luke 12:48). But how much *is* required? We'd often hear board members say, "How much is enough?" We couldn't answer that question for them; we could only try to answer it for ourselves.

Florence and I felt that it was important to keep Habitat's mission and goal in the forefront at all times. Together, we wrote a goal statement that the board signed off on. We printed this statement on the backs of business cards, invitations, and other DuPage Habitat for Humanity correspondence. It read:

Our Goal

> The fundamental goal of DuPage Habitat for Humanity is to provide homeownership opportunities to limited-income families or individuals, and to put the issue of permanent substandard rental housing on the minds and hearts of DuPage residents in such a powerful way that unattainable homeownership for these families or individuals becomes politically, socially, and religiously unacceptable.

Our written goal statement came out of my conviction that if we, as a society, truly believe that owning your own home is the American dream, then wouldn't it be un-American to deny that opportunity to those with limited incomes? Ownership is the antithesis of poverty.

Florence and I were now full-time volunteer servants being used by God to breathe life into the new organization. I was driven by a sense of urgency to move forward as fast as I could, and this was often met with some resistance by some of the board members. They all had full-time careers, and in most cases, families to raise still at home. Florence and I were at a point in our lives where we had chosen to do this work and volunteer full-time, and we explained that we didn't expect everyone to be as committed as we were. But whatever commitment they made, we expected them to fulfill it.

This philosophy—commit to what you can do, and see that commitment through—propelled us early on to set up the necessary committees—Site Selection, Family Selection, Construction, and Fundraising and Development—so that we would be ready to build after sites and properties were found and purchased. In affluent DuPage County, locating and buying sites to build on would turn out to be the biggest challenge—then, later, and even today.

Every Habitat affiliate in the United States (there were more than 1,200 of them at the time—today, there are 2,300) is responsible for setting up and running its own operations. Each affiliate must find and purchase suitable building sites; locate, qualify, and select prospective homeowner families; do all the necessary fundraising to build the Habitat houses; and finally, plan, design, and construct (with both skilled and unskilled volunteers) the houses themselves. It's quite a job. We constantly felt that time was precious and a commodity that challenged us every day.

Florence and I had been convinced to jump in the deep end, but we weren't alone. We received a lot of moral support from Habitat headquarters as well as comprehensive training manuals and all of the necessary materials for starting an affiliate. While we may not have done this before, hundreds of others had gone before us—and we could learn through their experience. That made an amazing difference.

Florence and I had decided to introduce the manuals to the board members at our first meeting. This would be a "baptism of fire" for each of them. After explaining the various committees that Habitat affiliates maintain, I asked the board members to take a leap of faith and commit to a committee of their choice. Most were eager to begin, but after that first meeting a few did not return. Eventually, we would consistently have between twelve and fifteen board members, and we were excited about the strong, successful people who had chosen to take on this commitment.

Of course, many of our strong members also had strong opinions with significant egos that sometimes got in the way of getting board business done. One night before a board meeting I posted a sign on the door to the meeting room. It read, "Tonight, please check your ego at the door. Thank you." The sign helped (at least that night) but I did need to be more patient. After all, none of the board members had experienced what Florence and I had in Americus and Barahona. Nor had they spent time getting inducted by the master himself, Millard Fuller, the charismatic and hard-working founder of Habitat for Humanity International.

In March, the *Chicago Tribune* ran an article titled "Helping Hands with Hammers." The piece described how Florence and I were starting a DuPage County Habitat presence, and helped us recruit volunteers and begin the necessary fund-raising efforts to launch the affiliate. The article also publicized our next two informational meetings about Habitat, both of which attracted about one hundred people. As we began to make ripples in the county, more people came forward to help row the Habitat boat—and not always gently.

We were blessed early on with leaders who really got things rolling. Our board included members like John Wheeler, a local businessman who owned an insurance agency. John helped me locate possible building sites, and within a few months we were contemplating purchasing our first two individual home sites plus a larger three-acre site that we quickly named "Habitat Crossing."

Habitat Crossing would be our first multiple home or "cluster" site where we hoped to build six attractive new homes around a cul-de-sac and park. The artist's renderings were beautiful and I secretly thought this would be our first version of "Bailey Park."

Mac Airhart, president of Airhart Construction Company, was another board member who played a vital role in getting Habitat off the ground. He led the Construction Committee and helped put in place the teams required to start the construction process. Mac even donated employee hours to provide supervision for our first two houses. Ken Cook was one of his employees, and worked as the construction supervisor. Even though he had three small children at home, he also volunteered many hours of his own time on weekends and became very close to the first Habitat homeowners.

While I concentrated on the site selection and construction process, Florence worked with board members to set up the family selection process, write the first newsletter, and begin fundraising operations. Pat Mathis and Susan Karcher, two of our original board members, co-chaired the Family Committee. The seven-member committee was responsible for selecting possible homeowners and mentoring and supporting them throughout the home-building process and thereafter. In 1996, volunteers Jennifer True and Ann Mikols became co-chairs and dedicated endless hours to selecting and nurturing thirteen Habitat families throughout 1996 and 1997.

The Family Committee selected families using three criteria: financial need; current substandard housing; and ability to repay the mortgage. Our affiliate held three large application sessions in different locations throughout DuPage County that first year. We publicized each meeting through newspaper ads, flyers at public libraries, and church bulletin inserts. At the meetings, volunteers spoke about Habitat and the general application process; attendees were given applications and had two weeks to return the completed applications. On average, we had over one hundred people in attendance, and usually received about twenty-five returned applications which were either approved or rejected. Families whose written applications were approved received a "home visit" conducted by two committee members before receiving a recommendation from the Family Committee for final approval by the board of directors.

To keep volunteers, donors, and community members apprised of Habitat's progress, Florence also helped create a Habitat newsletter. One of our board members, Karen Hanke, owned a printing company and volunteered to edit and print the newsletter. Florence and I collected articles from other volunteers and Florence typed up the newsletter using PageMaker software; the first eight-page issue, *Building Up,* was sent out in October 1995 to about 1,000 people. Florence and I shared responsibility for the newsletter until 1997, when Wayne Hoffman, a retired high school English teacher, took over and wrote, edited, and prepared the mockup of each issue through 2002.

Of course nothing could happen without money, and we raised funds in a number of ways that first year and thereafter. We identified "Founders," people who agreed to donate $5,000 the first year, as well as "Carpenter's Club" members, who donated at least $100. We asked churches and corporations to be "House Sponsors," which required a donation of about $50,000 for each house. Board member Paulette Alshanski, the vice-president of a local bank, was a tireless fundraiser and helped organize donation requests from banks.

As Florence and I divided up responsibilities, we began to develop an amazing synergy where one and one added up not to two, but three. When I was single, making up a king-sized bed alone took several minutes. After I married Florence, we always made the bed together each morning, with her standing on one side and me on the other. The task took less than half the time and effort it would have before. *That* is synergy! (In fact, as I look back, this everyday example illustrates the impact that synergy had on what Florence and I accomplished together. One magazine article described our relationship as a "synergistic spiritual partnership." I think that says it all!)

Others marveled or lamented, depending on their viewpoint, at the progress we were making. But no matter how fast we raised funds, recruited volunteers, and interviewed prospective family homeowners, nothing was going to happen until we acquired our first site.

So I set out, sometimes alone and sometimes with John Wheeler, traveling the side streets of the county looking for empty lots for sale and talking to realtors day after day. Nothing seemed to be in a price range we could afford. From talking with other Habitat affiliates in the Chicago area, we knew that even most small vacant lots were well beyond the $30,000 figure we'd set our sights on.

I met with municipal staff officials throughout the county, trying to locate condemned or abandoned houses, but most told me that I was probably too late. Most municipalities implemented vigorous enforcement programs that sold these homes to speculators or builders; they were then torn down to be replaced by considerably larger, more expensive homes that elevated home values and were welcomed by most of the surrounding neighbors.

One day in the spring of 1995, Mike Baker, who worked for the building department of West Chicago, a community west of Wheaton, called to give me a heads-up. There was a home on Parkside Avenue in a nice but modest neighborhood that had been boarded up and abandoned. The home had been leased by an absentee homeowner, but when the most recent renters had left unannounced one night with back rent due, the owner apparently got fed up and abandoned the property. Because of the house's condition, most home builders would consider it to be a typical teardown. The yard was overgrown, and the house itself was in bad shape. As the city could not locate the property owner, however, it was not able to take any legal action on the property. Mike thought the homeowner might be in the Atlanta area and gave me his name.

I began my "wing and a prayer" mission to see if I could find him. I searched recorded tax rolls and other records, and called anyone I could think of who might have an idea of where I might look for him. (This was in the days before google.com!) By a coincidence (or miracle, if you prefer), I finally located his place of employment. When I called there, the person who answered the phone told me that he was almost never there. Yet that day, I was able to reach him.

His voice was soft, and he struck me as a caring person. I explained the Habitat process, which he had never heard of, but seemed to appreciate. At first he said he wasn't interested in selling the house. But I couldn't stop myself. For some urgent reason, I decided to make him a modest cash offer for what I considered to be the value of the lot. As the house was in total disrepair, I said we would probably rehab the house with our volunteers. Instead of tearing it down, the way any other buyer would, we would turn his home into a dream home for a new, wonderful family. He liked the idea, and to my surprise, accepted my offer on the spot. The two of us were able to exchange enough information to plan on closing the deal in escrow, which allowed us to do it by mail.

There was only one problem. Even though I felt moved to do this when I had the chance, our affiliate had no funds, nor did I have the approval of the DuPage Habitat board of directors. After much discussion about the fact that we were moving too fast for some of its members, the board approved the purchase—after I asked for forgiveness as I had preempted the permission process.

While driving back and forth to the Parkside location I had noticed a vacant lot for sale on Washington Street that turned out to be in our price range. The board members felt comfortable in accepting a short-term loan from the RJN Foundation to purchase both properties. I felt confident that Habitat could repay the loan soon—so confident that Florence and I offered a no-interest loan to Habitat for the purchase of a large parcel of property across from the St. Andrew Lutheran Church on Geneva Road in West Chicago that would be known as Habitat Crossing. (Eventually, with successful fundraising, all of the loans were paid back.)

Besides Florence and I, other volunteers worked to set up church meetings to recruit potential donors and volunteers. Glenn Gilbert started out as a volunteer and organized the Church Development Committee, and became a board member in 1996. He assisted Florence and me when we presented to local churches—we quickly found that churches were our greatest partners. Steve Timmer was another Church Development Committee volunteer who helped raise funds and joined the board in 1997.

Through meetings and outreach, we built a database of several thousand people. Dorothy Gorton-Murdock, one of our initial board members, donated a comprehensive database software program to manage all this new information. Even though she worked full-time, she would spend several of her lunch hours teaching Florence and Angi Perri how to use the database software so we could keep track of our donors and volunteers. That database supported DuPage Habitat for Humanity's efforts for many years.

Angi was our first full-time Habitat employee, and responsible for various office administration tasks like answering the telephone, greeting visitors, preparing board materials, working with volunteers, and maintaining communication among committee chairs. Florence had sole responsibility for the financial accounting activities for the affiliate for some time. This included the usual depositing checks and paying bills, plus governmental reporting. It was a Godsend to her when Norma Hamill came on board in 1996 and volunteered two days a week to assist Florence with her bookkeeping responsibilities. As committee chairs approved expense invoices, the invoices were routed to Norma to pay. Florence recorded financial donations and Norma wrote thank-you notes and filed necessary paperwork. Many other board members and volunteers played essential roles in the success of our new Habitat affiliate.

Once Mac Airhart and his professional crew inspected the boarded-up house on Parkside, we were sure we could rebuild and refinish the home both outside and inside instead of tearing it down and starting from scratch. On June 10, 1995, we held DuPage Habitat for Humanity's first groundbreaking ceremony. Almost one hundred volunteers gathered in the center of our newly acquired vacant lot on Washington Street in West Chicago. While people balanced on the uneven ground covered by newly mowed weeds and crabgrass, I stood at the podium and gave thanks for this new ministry in DuPage County. I believe all in attendance shared the same exuberance and excitement that Florence and I felt about being part of this historical day.

After taking many photos and being interviewed by the press, we assembled on the street with a West Chicago police escort. Our proud banners waved in the light breeze as we walked the four blocks to the Parkside house, where more volunteers were waiting to celebrate opening day for Habitat for Humanity in DuPage County.

Dumpsters were lined up, stacks of gloves were awaiting their "hammer swingers," and we had a refreshment table to keep people happy and a first aid table to keep them healthy. Experienced carpenters had brought their own tool belts and tools, but we also had hammers, sledgehammers, and crowbars for volunteers to use to assist in the rehab. After giving thanks for the opportunity to create this new home and praying for safety for everyone there, we broke into groups and were assigned a supervisor. Volunteers worked on the outside of the house, tearing down the front porch and prying away the old siding and roof. Inside, others took out the rotted kitchen cabinets and ripped off the old drywall. We were fortunate that many volunteers had brought their own tools, but in less than a month, we would amass enough donated hammers, saws, wrenches, screwdrivers, and other tools for all volunteers to use at our building sites.

The process of gutting the inside of the house and removing the shingles and siding from the outside of the house was underway. We filled the dumpsters quickly, unaware that the impact of that day would eventually be heard throughout DuPage County and later and somewhat sadly, even in the federal courts.

While the working committees were getting off the ground, I was concentrating on what I hoped would be our first home cluster project in West Chicago, across from the St. Andrew Lutheran Church. One of my first clients when I started RJN Environmental in 1975 was a consulting engineering firm, Pavia-Marting, Inc., located in a neighboring community. One of the owners, Dale Marting, and I had remained friends throughout the years, and Dale was a member of St. Andrew's board of directors.

Eventually DuPage Habitat purchased the property from the church. This site would become known as Habitat Crossing by our affiliate. Thanks to both Dale's influence and the support of Pastor Fred Reklau, the church board became excited about the project and the possibility of partnering with Habitat to help build the new homes right across the street from the church.

We already had artist's renderings and layouts and elevation drawings created for the attractive, modest ranch homes which would all have three bedrooms and two-car attached garages. The property, however, had no access to a wastewater sewer line, and before we could build, a new 400-foot sewer line would have to be constructed to hook up to an existing sewer main across Geneva Road. Florence and I quickly prepared a grant application and submitted it to DuPage County, requesting a $440,000 grant for the construction of the new sewer line. We received county approval for the grant.

The next step was to get approval from the City of West Chicago to annex the property from the county and rezone it for residential use. This step required a public hearing and approval by both the West Chicago Planning Commission and the West Chicago City Council. We arranged to have a neighborhood meeting at the church where we would share all of the information we had about Habitat along with the drawings and other exhibits that showed that the houses would all be similar to and in character with the surrounding neighborhood. We intended to introduce the neighbors to what we thought would be a welcome use of a vacant lot—it would be transformed into six beautiful new homes for first-time homeowner families.

We expected excitement. What we heard instead were cries of fear, hatred, and loathing—all directed at us. The neighbors believed that we would destroy their neighborhood with Habitat homes. No matter how hard we tried to explain that the homes would physically fit in with the character and appearance of other homes in the neighborhood, the people attending the meeting remained unconvinced. Although we were in church, they screamed at us that we were building low-income housing for families who did not deserve those homes. "Those families are poor because they deserve to be!" "Nobody ever gave *me* anything." "I like the idea of Habitat, but you can't build here." "Those families won't take care of their homes." We heard statements like these, and worse.

Some spoke emotionally about their decision to leave their urban neighborhoods in Chicago because of the "redlining" process that allowed unscrupulous realtors to scare people into selling their homes by convincing them that if they stayed, they would lose most of their property value. Some of the neighbors here in West Chicago had real concern that Habitat houses would somehow lower their property values. Nothing we said about the difference between a particular urban neighborhood in Chicago and six new Habitat homes in a suburban setting changed their mind. They were afraid of what might happen here in suburbia.

Some people did speak about how wonderful Habitat was. The consensus, however, was that we should build the homes someplace else—and "not in my back yard." For us Habitat volunteers, it was our first, but not our last, experience with the "NIMBY" phenomenon.

Yet, we were not swayed. We knew that our cause was just and necessary; we simply needed to win the neighbors over. If we could just get them to learn more about Habitat's success throughout the country it would quell their fears, right? Or so we thought.

The public hearing process before the West Chicago Planning Commission dragged on for several months. Hundreds of people attended each session of the continuing hearing process as we presented spokespersons, church representatives, and newly selected families who provided evidence about the merits of Habitat. The neighbors on the other side organized, hired legal counsel, and essentially refused to hear anything we had to say. A year later, the city gave in to the vocal residents and denied the project. (At the time of the writing of this book, the Habitat Crossing site is still a vacant lot, never built on, and never realizing its potential.)

At this point, some of the Habitat volunteers who had joined Florence and me in this fight moved on, but many returned to continue to not only build new homes, but to raise the consciousness level of the community about the need for Habitat homes. Although I felt that Habitat Crossing should have been built and wasn't, I believed we should try again in another location to build a cluster of Habitat homes. With a cluster, Habitat families could live close to each other and be able to rely on each other instead of being scattered over the thirty square miles of DuPage County. Cluster building also provided "economy of scale," lowering the cost of each home.

This was particularly important as nothing in DuPage County was cheap to build.

In the meantime, our newly formed affiliate was making great progress in finishing our first home on Parkside. On Washington Street, our second home was going up and would be finished during our first year; a corporate sponsorship from the Rubbermaid Corporation helped make that happen. Meeting and getting to know the two families that would move into these homes made our work more real—now it wasn't just about the idea of building houses, but about the actual people who would help build and live in these homes.

To help plan for the coming year, in January 1996, we held our first DuPage Habitat board retreat. January is usually "down time" for the hotel industry, and we were fortunate that a local hotel donated one of it's ballrooms and provided a free box lunch to our board members for the retreat. Habitat may be a volunteer organization but it still has to be run efficiently to be successful and sustainable.

At the retreat, I used a facilitation technique I developed while running RJN Group. We met as a group and brainstormed all "items of interest and concern," determined which were the most significant items, and then broke into small discussion groups to talk about each item.

After lunch, we reconvened to share the outcomes from each group. The Construction Committee discussion group found an innovative answer to a major concern. DuPage Habitat had about a dozen retired men who volunteered as supervisors at the construction sites on weekdays and Saturdays. As supervisors, they were trained to give a beginning safety talk and provide direction during the day as well as working on the house. However, many volunteer workers with questions sometimes wasted a lot of time looking for a supervisor as he looked like everyone else on the site.

We needed a way to make the supervisors stand out, and the board voted to create the Orange Hats. We bought sharp-looking neon orange caps with the DuPage Habitat logo for site supervisors to wear on the job. This helped volunteers identify the supervisors, and created a special bond among the construction supervisors. It became a source of pride to be an Orange Hat.

One of our first Orange Hats, Art Roberts, volunteered for Habitat since the beginning. He started as a construction supervisor for our first Habitat house, but he didn't stop at construction. He took the time to build a caring relationship with the each of the Habitat homeowners and their families. He remains an active Orange Hat today, participating in early construction planning and continuing to provide solid leadership on the committee. Other long-time Orange Hats include Dick Mylander, Ray Ramage, and Joe Benigni.

Kevin Schuele also started out as a volunteer on the Construction Committee, and in 1996, we hired him as a full-time employee of Habitat. We built twelve houses in two years, and Kevin coordinated all construction activities until he returned to graduate school in 1998.

Later in 1996, we received another corporate sponsorship from Target to build a home in Lombard, and a group of churches came together in another part of the county to build a duplex townhome in Westmont, southeast of Wheaton. The next year, a good friend and a "give-back" builder, Perry Bigelow, generously donated a site in one of his subdivisions in Aurora for a new four-unit townhome building.

As we continued to acquire additional lots, I thought that local companies could be a great source of both volunteers and funds for our building sites. I agreed to chair the Corporate Donation Committee and made presentations to several area companies about the benefits of a "Corporate Work Day" at a

Habitat house construction site. I knew from my own experience and from published studies that when employees share
an out-of-office experience, they form bonds of friendship that
enhance their existing work relationships.

After convincing corporate officers to accept the challenge,
I'd tell them the suggested donation was ten dollars per volunteer hour. Corporate officers were often surprised by there being
a cost to participate. "But we're building the house for you!"
they'd say. "Yes," I'd reply. "And we provide the supervision,
supplies, tools, insurance, and platform for your employees to
share this experience." Over the years, more than fifty companies participated in the Corporate Work Day, and many came
back more than once when they witnessed increased employee
effectiveness and efficiency back at the office.

In the summer of 1996, we also had an opportunity to purchase twenty already-improved, vacant lots in Glendale Heights.
This could be the cluster of Habitat homes I'd envisioned. In
anticipation of building all of these homes, several hundred
volunteers had been working on different tasks, including
holding fundraising events, organizing church support, planning the new homes, and holding family application meetings
throughout the county that would lead to the selection of new
homeowners for all these new houses.

I believed that the Glendale Heights project could help
create lasting local acceptance of Habitat for Humanity and
quell the fears of the NIMBY supporters. But fear is a strong
emotion. It can be used to paralyze people and blind them to
what is possible and positive, not only for someone else but for
themselves.

This was brought home to me at a meeting with a DuPage
County board official when I tried to explain why cluster homes
made more sense because of economy of scale and the well-
being of the families involved. Apparently, political pressure

was mounting to keep us from building more than one home at a time. I can still hear his words echoing in my head. He shook his head at me, ignoring the material I'd brought. "You shall build one house at a time in DuPage County." I left the meeting angry and frustrated. Our rights were being violated, but what could we do about it?

At that time I was also working on a new multi-house site in an older section of Wheaton that we thought would be perfect for Habitat. The area needed new curbs, storm sewers, and sidewalks; we obtained a DuPage County HOME Grant commitment, which provides federal funds to help install the necessary infrastructure. The six new homes would fill in an incomplete "dead end" part of the street.

Again, the drawings we prepared for the houses of Project Summit were beautiful. Reverend Andre Allen, pastor of the local Baptist church, was excited about the opportunity to partner with Habitat. He arranged to have a neighborhood meeting in the church hall downstairs where the neighbors could come and learn about the new houses and improvements to the neighborhood. He was confident that we would proceed, but nothing could have been further from the truth.

Once again, we were faced with loathing, fear of the unknown, and a refusal to look beyond that fear and trust Habitat's mission. We were later denied approval by the Wheaton City Council on a technicality and another $500,000 grant was lost. As of this day, the neighborhood still lacks sidewalks and drainage improvements.

At DuPage Habitat, we hadn't given up. We were still working on what we hoped would be our banner project—the twenty existing, improved lots in Glendale Heights. We requested grant money from the Illinois Housing Development Authority to help us launch the project. Glendale Heights is a DuPage County suburb a few miles east of Wheaton where our split-level design homes with two-car attached garages would fit in with the existing neighborhood.

Much to our surprise, though, instead of us being treated like every other builder in Glendale Heights, the village board decided to stop us because of newly organized opposition from neighbors in the area where our scattered lots were located. We agreed to build only four homes at first to show how successful they would be. We were confident that after that, the village and the neighbors would be comfortable with more Habitat homes in the area. After completing these four homes, however, the village refused to issue building permits on the remaining lots. Apparently in their minds, building more Habitat houses for limited-income homeowners would "destroy" the surrounding neighborhood.

After long discussions with the DuPage Habitat Board, we decided to accept help from a legal firm and civil rights groups in Chicago. Late in 1998, we filed suit against the Village of Glendale Heights in federal court on the grounds that our Fourteenth Amendment rights were being violated, and that we were being deprived of equal treatment under the law. After several years, we finally went to trial in Chicago in January 2001 in federal court. The judge eventually ruled against us.

It was a loss in more ways than one. The leadership at DuPage Habitat was spent, exhausted, and did not appeal. Perhaps that was a mistake, but we will never know. Yet while I was caught up fighting these battles, Florence, Kevin Schuele, and many other committed and dedicated volunteers kept the affiliate on a productive course as homes continued to be built. Despite the challenges, we would celebrate life and hope for the future with the new Habitat homeowner families. It would be getting to know these families that would give Florence and me joy, fulfillment, and an even greater reward than we had expected.

Above: Millard and Linda Fuller, co-founders of Habitat for Humanity International, with Florence and Dick taken in Millard's office during our visit in October 1994.

Right: Dick and Linda Fuller get reacquainted during the "Jimmy Carter Weekend" in May 1998, in Americus, Georgia.

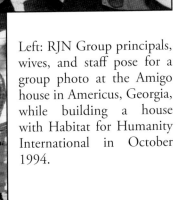

Left: RJN Group principals, wives, and staff pose for a group photo at the Amigo house in Americus, Georgia, while building a house with Habitat for Humanity International in October 1994.

Above: RJN Group principals Al Hollenbeck, Steve Maney, and Hugh Kelso work with Dick to secure the roof braces.

Right: Florence and Dick nailing shingles to the roof of the Habitat House.

Left: Scott Rebman and Steve Maney helping each other measure and cut plywood.

Above: There was no building crane on site, so everyone helped lift the roof trusses to the four men on top.

Below: A group shot looking through a framed window on our last day on the job. Our group bonding experience was a huge success.

Barahona,
Dominican Republic

Right: Climbing aboard our transportation to and from the job site each day. The locals called it a "gua gua," or limo.

Below: Steve and Chris, Habitat for Humanity International partners in Barahona—a committed, unique couple.

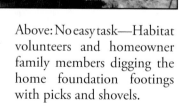

Above: No easy task—Habitat volunteers and homeowner family members digging the home foundation footings with picks and shovels.

Left: Dick offering his civil engineering expertise at the construction site.

Right: Dick (looking down) passes a pail of wet concrete to Florence as part of the "bucket brigade" used to get concrete to the roof of the Habitat house under construction.

Left: Florence with two prospective Habitat homeowners in Barahona after a hard day at work.

Below: Our host family in Barahona, the Don Gabriel family (Ella is sitting next to her father).

Volunteering becomes a way of life

Nogajs bring Habitat habit to work in county

By Julie Busch

After a recent workday at the first DuPage Habitat for Humanity project, founders Dick and Florence Nogaj reviewed their progress.

Everyone had already left the site after seven hours of work, where they had torn away siding, gutted a kitchen, and cleaned up the back yard.

"We stood there and just looked around," Florence said. "It looked so different than it did just hours before. We could actually see the families living there. It looked like somebody's back yard."

It's this kind of transformation, both to the house and to the volunteers who participate, that draws people, including the Nogajs (pronounced no-jay), to Habitat for Humanity.

"We have opened the door," said Florence, 47. "We've been blessed with 'can do' people who want to get involved."

After launching the ministry in DuPage County in November, the Nogajs, of Wheaton, have found numerous people joining the non-profit ministry.

Earlier this month, the first project began in West Chicago, with the renovation of a boarded-up house. A second house will be built in the city later this summer.

At a work session last weekend, three families selected to live in the planned homes showed up to begin their 500 hours of "sweat equity," required in order to be eligible.

"They need to start giving us input with colors and other things," Dick, 57, said.

The families now live in roach-infested apartments in West Chicago, one with no working refrigerator. They will serve as model families.

See NOGAJ on Page 5

(Photo courtesy of the Nogajs)

Dick and Florence Nogaj started DuPage Habitat for Humanity and found something meaningful they could do together.

Above: One of the first local newspaper articles in June 1995 announcing the arrival of Habitat for Humanity in DuPage County, Illinois. (Reprinted with permission of the Wheaton Sun.)

Right: Art Roberts (far right), DuPage HFH supervising demolition at the first project in 1995.

Below: Dick and Florence with Kevin Schuele, DuPage HFH construction manager, attending a Habitat home dedication in March 1997.

Below right: Dick's dear friend, Ed Younger, at a DHFH home dedication in 1997.

Above: Dick speaking to well wishers at the Zavala family Habitat home dedication on September 28, 1995.

Left: Before—an abandoned house and a public eyesore.

Below: After—a bonus for the neighborhood and a beautiful place for the Zavala family to live and grow.

A few DuPage Habitat families:
Above: Manuel and Guadalupe Fernandez with Dick (far right) and representatives from the Rubbermaid Corporation which sponsored construction of this Habitat home. (Reprinted with permission from Blair-Jensen Photography)

Left: Alex and Elsie Vela signing the title to the new Habitat home they will share with their eight children.

Right: Florence speaking with Chi and Kim Nguyen and their four children at their Habitat home dedication in 1998. Chet Staples (plaid shirt) became the second board president of DHFH.

Chapter Five

BREAD, SALT, AND WINE—AND THE KEYS TO YOUR HOME

THE REJECTION OF THREE single-family multi-home projects—not to mention what they would have meant to the families who would have lived there and the growth of the affiliate they would have caused—weighed heavily on my mind. The work I'd been doing for Habitat had been like an intense boxing match for the past two years. The knockdowns and "get-ups" were fast and furious, and I was spent.

The last of the three rejections, confirmed by, in my opinion, a wrongful decision by the federal court, was the most difficult to accept. I couldn't believe that we hadn't won. Our cause was just and right, and yet the village and the federal court had ruled against us. I felt I had failed by refusing to recognize the many voices, even from Habitat International, that had told us not to build where we were not wanted. But I believed that our work shouldn't only be doing what was popular or accepted, but doing what was right. It was right for the families who had been selected for new homes, and who had already worked and met their sweat equity requirements for their own homes. In some cases, families continued to return to worksites to help build homes for others—even after exceeding the sweat equity hours required for their own homes. (Married couples provided 500 hours of sweat equity; single parents, 250 hours.)

Being knocked down a third time in Glendale Heights felt like strike three. Yet I was reminded of something my parents had said to me as a child:

> *You are beaten to earth? Well, well what's that?*
> *Come up with a smiling face.*
> *It's nothing against you to fall down flat—*
> *But to lie there—that's a disgrace.*

That memory motivated me to get up, stop feeling sorry for myself, and recognize how much we had accomplished. Even dealing with the ever-present NIMBY mentality, we were still on a course that was bringing hope and happiness into the lives of new Habitat families. We might not be going as fast as I wanted, but we were making progress. And I knew that I needed to focus on my relationship with Florence. Our work and the time and emotional effort involved were straining our new partnership and marriage. If I was to accomplish the dream of a Bailey Park as George and Mary did in *It's a Wonderful Life*, I knew I wasn't going to do it without Florence.

Both of us realized that we needed to return to the roots of our relationship and use more of the tools we had learned early in the Imago process. Finding time for ourselves and for our extended families was an ongoing challenge. We were a blended family with five adult children between the two of us; in addition, we'd eventually have eleven grandchildren. We worked hard to keep them all in our lives, and also stay close to both of our aging mothers as well as our siblings. We decided that we would always keep all of our loved ones close to our hearts and even if we could not be with them in person, we could be with them in spirit.

I wasn't taking this journey alone. It was also about Florence and her needs, and it was my responsibility to stay focused on the part I played in that process. So we brushed up on our Imago skills and set out to find new Imago counselors in the area. We attended many sessions with certified Imago counselor Leo Dhont. We had learned these skills before, but we needed to make them a habit again. I worked on actively listening to Florence, mirroring back what I heard, and expressing empathy for how I would feel if I were Florence. And she did the same for me.

One of the core issues we faced was that we were still living in the townhome that I owned when we got married. Florence had sold her condo and moved in with me after the wedding. Our original plan had been to sell both of our places and then get a place together, but we'd put searching for a new place on hold because we were so busy with Habitat. Yet when friends and families would visit and reminisce about previous family holiday celebrations, it bothered Florence. She felt—and I realized—that we were living with a lot of "ghosts" by staying in my place. There's a certain irony here. I'd been so focused on helping other people become homeowners I hadn't realized how important it was to Florence that we have our own home together.

After attending counseling sessions together, I finally realized how crucial it was for us to have a place that was truly ours. We sold my townhome and purchased a nice two-bedroom end unit townhome in the same subdivision in November 1998. We remodeled the house together and it became a reflection of our shared life instead of my previous one. At the time, we had no idea we would end up spending most of our time outside of Wheaton in just a few years.

While Florence and I reconnected, our Habitat work continued at a demanding pace. Over the first three years, the affiliate built sixteen homes throughout DuPage County. Habitat built several homes in West Chicago and both officials and residents got to know the outstanding Habitat families that had worked to own their own homes.

About a year after we were denied the right to build several single family homes at one site, I received a call from a staff official in West Chicago about a large tract of land in a residential area. The land was already zoned and subdivided for six homes, and the owner had decided he would not be able to develop it. The city official told me the owner might be interested in selling to us at a reasonable price.

When I visited the site, I found it would be perfect for six new Habitat homes, each with a large back yard. The homes would be similar to the others on the block. I spoke with some neighbors about the possibility of building there, and they were unbelievably encouraging and positive. NIMBY didn't seem to be an issue in that neighborhood. Later, in 1998, we held groundbreaking ceremonies at the site that came to be called the "Oak Street Community." We completed the homes the following year, six new families moved in, and with the new addition the neighborhood was now completely built out. At last, we'd built a cluster of homes with no NIMBY and no resistance. Oak Street Community became the "Yes, we can" neighborhood, reminding me of the RJN motto, "We'll find a way."

For me, Oak Street was a personal vindication. It was proof that if you get up off the floor, keep moving forward, and focus on your purpose and message, change *is* possible. That change happened because of the many volunteers, board members, and the Habitat families who never gave up—and changed the way people thought of Habitat.

We also now had full-time staff who helped us with day-to-day activities. Kevin Schuele, a Wheaton resident in his early 20s, had started out as a volunteer before he was hired as our construction supervisor. He worked tirelessly with me and the volunteers to oversee twenty homes from groundbreaking to dedication. Kevin later went on to achieve his calling as a minister and continued to help build lives as well as homes.

Marilyn Michaud became Florence's right-hand person for all the day-to-day administrative responsibilities. Marilyn was invaluable not only to the affiliate but to Florence personally. While working as a full-time volunteer for Habitat, Florence was somehow able to finish her undergraduate degree at Elmhurst College as well.

Seeing the houses built from the ground up was amazing. Even more enriching, however, was coming to know—and love—twenty families who purchased and worked for their Habitat homes. Our first home dedication ceremony will always remain closest to my heart. When we found the house on Parkside, it was a drab, boarded-up, one-story frame house with badly peeling white paint, missing and decayed roof shingles, and broken windows. Overgrown shrubs hid the front of the home, broken gutters hung from the house, and the yard was little more than dirt and patchy grass.

At the dedication ceremony, the house had been transformed into a freshly sided home with new windows, a new roof and gutters, and a freshly poured sidewalk. Shiny dark green shutters that matched the dark green front door, trimmed shrubs, pots full of pink flowers, and a yard full of new grass welcomed Carolina and Alejandro Zavala, and their three children, Vincent, fifteen; Joey, ten; and Alejandra, three. Carolina was a large woman with an even bigger heart, and she had a great smile. While she worked fulltime, every Saturday she would show up to the worksite with a cup of coffee for Ken

Cook, the construction supervisor. She worked alongside the volunteers every Saturday, doing any job requested of her. Her older children, especially Vincent, also volunteered and got to know many of the volunteers at the work site.

Caroline's husband, Alejandro was a roofer and had to work every weekend at his regular job. But when the time came to put the house's shingles on, he brought a crew of his coworkers—who all volunteered their time—to do the work.

Florence welcomed everyone to the dedication ceremony, and several others spoke briefly including Art Roberts and West Chicago city council member Dave Sabathne. Dave had always been a strong Habitat supporter. The following year, he would be the only council member to vote for Habitat Crossing in West Chicago. I was stunned when in his remarks, Dave referenced none other than *It's a Wonderful Life*. He referred to me as a "modern-day George Bailey," and the forces trying to stop us as "Mr. Potter." I had never told him of my fondness for the movie or how it had touched me.

Then, completely on his own, he lifted the tradition from the movie about the "basket of essentials" the homeowners received before being given the keys to their house. Dave handed Carolina "bread, so that this house will never know hunger; salt, that life may always have flavor; and wine, that joy and prosperity may follow you forever." The ceremony of the basket of essentials became a part of every home dedication by DuPage Habitat for Humanity from that day on.

Carolina spoke briefly, wiping tears from her eyes as she thanked everyone for their work on her new home. I then presented her with the keys, and she cut the ribbon that hung across the front porch. She and her family walked into the house they now owned as I led the crowd in a cry of "Oyée!" This was the phrase I'd heard Millard Fuller say so often—it was the cry of celebration that he brought back from Zaire, where the concept of Habitat for Humanity was born.

While Florence and I got to know all of the Habitat families, we became especially close to some of them. Manuel and Guadalupe Fernandez and their children, Lupita, sixteen; Thalia, two; and Abraham, six months, purchased the second home Habitat built, on Washington Street, and moved in in October 1995. Manuel worked at a printing firm, and Guadalupe worked for a paper cup manufacturer. While they both worked full-time, they were never able to save enough for a down payment. This time, however, they put in over 1,000 hours of sweat equity as their down payment while helping to build their own Habitat house.

Many years later, Florence and I were invited to their home for a Christmas dinner, and the family was reminiscing about how they had helped build their home. Lupita would hand Manuel 2x4 inch wall hangers as Manuel hammered nails into them to put them into place. They had worked next to executives from the Rubbermaid Corporation who came from Ohio to sponsor and build this home with the Fernandez family.

Lupita went on to finish high school with high honors and had earned her college degree, and Thalia and Abraham had grown into fine young musicians. They serenaded Florence and me with Christmas melodies. Florence and I were also overwhelmed with joy to see how happy Manuel and Guadalupe were. They had overcome earlier obstacles in their marriage and were now a stronger couple. Volunteer partner families had "adopted" Manuel and Guadalupe, just as other Habitat families received similar nurturing experiences. That night, the breaking of bread, the laughter of children, and the loving spirit that dwelled in all of us was our reward for the work we had started years ago.

Every Habitat family has its own story, but some have always stood out in my mind. In 1998, about one hundred volunteers gathered for a home dedication in West Chicago for Chi and Kim Nguyen and their four children. About twenty-five years earlier, Chi, a pilot for the South Vietnamese army, was shot down in North Vietnam. Over the next several years he managed to make it back to South Vietnam, and married his childhood sweetheart, Kim. They had two children in Vietnam before immigrating to the United States after the Vietnam War, and had two more children here, settling in the Wheaton area.

Chi worked full-time as a waiter, and Kim worked for a catering company, but because of their low-paying jobs, they could only afford a one-bedroom apartment. With four children, they had to move every year; the landlord would evict them each time due to building occupancy codes for overcrowding. Their oldest daughter, Hang, was sixteen and brilliant, but she suffered from having to move from school to school every year. Her dream was to go to college and major in pharmacology.

At the Nguyens' home dedication, Habitat volunteers gathered on the driveway and in the yard singing songs and thanking Coldwell Banker for its corporate sponsorship. Before the key-passing ceremony and the basket of essentials, the pastor from St. Mary's Catholic Church in West Chicago spoke. Father Vern Arseneau, always a staunch supporter of Habitat, had already witnessed many "NIMBY" meetings in West Chicago where fear manifested itself in words like, "Not here," "Stay out," and "Never."

At the dedication, however, he spoke about a new day of reconciliation, not just in West Chicago but in the healing of a nation as we remembered the Vietnam War and this wonderful family who had emigrated from Vietnam to remind us that we are still one body of people who all belong to the same God. Father Arseneau's speech was heard not only by Habitat volunteers but many of the Nguyens' new neighbors who had joined us for the day of celebration of new life symbolized by a new, safe place the Nguyens would call home.

As years have passed, we have often visited the Nguyen family at their home. More recently, we stopped by to see Hang at her place of employment, a local pharmacy in Wheaton. After graduating with honors from West Chicago High School, she received a scholarship with help from the RJN Foundation and attended Benedictine University and later Midwestern University where she received her Doctor of Pharmacology degree. Florence and I overflow with pride as we watch the Nguyen family, who were saved from the carnage of the Vietnam War and are now making a difference in their surroundings in DuPage County.

For some of these families, Habitat was that first "hand up" experience that most of us are lucky enough to receive from parents, friends, or others. Don't listen if someone tells you that he is self-made and no one ever gave him anything. This was often the sentiment we heard from NIMBY people, who wrongly believed that Habitat was a hand-out, not a hand up. There's another great American myth that we are a society of bootstrap success. Nonsense. Our society is based on and flourishes because of hand-up success for all of us—no exceptions.

With the Habitat hand-up process and their newfound stability, some families were able to move on—to marry, get better jobs, and improve their educations. Some have even been able to sell their houses back to Habitat so they could be resold to other families. While they may no longer be Habitat families, we still remember their impact on our lives.

One of the most powerful and lasting family experiences for us was meeting Alex and Elsie Vela and their family of eight children. At the end of one of the family application meetings, a handsome Latino man in his forties approached me and asked if there was anything we could do for him and his family. He had lost his job and was about to be evicted because the bank was foreclosing on their home. As I spoke with him, I told him I didn't know what we could do with such a large family on such short notice. We had no home available, and I didn't think we could help him but I asked him to submit the application and information to the Family Selection Committee.

Several months later, we were preparing to build the Oak Street Community, and found that one of the lots could be suitable for a raised ranch with four bedrooms to accommodate a large family. I didn't think such a family was in the selection process at the time, but on a weekend at home with Florence, I suddenly was overcome with thoughts of the man who had approached me several months back. I couldn't recall his name, but Florence and I talked and prayed and rushed back to the office to see if we could find that application. We went through files and files that Saturday afternoon and finally found a file that described a family that size.

On Monday, Florence and I called the Velas and asked if we could visit them at their home in Glendale Heights. Fortunately, they had not been evicted yet. After we met them, we decided that they would be a perfect Habitat family. The Velas, devout Catholics, were humble and sincere. We'd later find out that Elsie and Alex had prayed together every day asking for a solution to losing their home. Two weeks after they received the eviction notice, Elsie saw the announcement in their local paper about the family application meeting. She thought this might be the answer to their prayers.

We talked about how we could get them enough time until a Habitat home could be built. Their modest home was clean, but very sparse. They'd had to sell furniture—including their beds—to buy food. Florence and I came back to the office and went to work. We contacted the foreclosure company and the attorneys involved in the process. We finally arranged to speak in front of the foreclosure judge in Wheaton, and asked for a foreclosure stay based on the promise of a Habitat house. The judge agreed to the stay, Alex got a temporary job through one of the Habitat volunteers, and the Vela family began to get back on its feet.

The Velas continue to live in their beautiful house on Oak Street, and they are involved in both their church and their community. Alex has excelled in his new career in sales and management, and their eight children have done well in school. They often return as a family to volunteer for Habitat. Habitat was the answer to their prayers at that time, and today their family continues to blossom.

The Oak Street Community cluster of homes and families was the first multiple single-family homes built at one location and was welcomed by the neighbors in that part of West Chicago. But in the summer of 1996, before Oak Street was built, Perry Bigelow, president and founder of Bigelow Homes, was completing a subdivision a few miles west on Butterfield Road near Aurora, on the western edge of DuPage County. He donated a site, complete with concrete slab and infrastructure for a four-unit townhome building that would later be named "Project Dawn," to DuPage Habitat. This four-unit building would also fall outside of the "one house at a time" order that we received from politicians within the county.

While DuPage County has a population of about one million people living in thirty-four incorporated municipalities, there's also a fairly large unincorporated area that falls under the county's jurisdiction (as opposed to a city or village). The four-unit townhome already had a building permit, thank God. This was during the height of the NIMBY activity and we were worried that the neighborhood might try to stop us again. It didn't take long for the local press to find out about this pending Habitat project. During our years with the affiliate, Florence and I learned how some of the press had a nose for controversy and seldom missed a chance to "stir the pot."

One of the big problems we had with the press and the "NIMBYs" was that they stereotyped Habitat as "low-income housing" providers. This conjured up negative images of public housing that is rented, not owned, and is often rundown and crime-ridden. Habitat housing couldn't have been more different. With Habitat, we built housing for limited-income working families that was in character with the neighborhood. Most of our DuPage County homes were modest split levels with two-car attached garages, homes you'd find in any local suburb. These homes were owned, not rented, and the mortgages were held by Habitat, not by an unknown bank.

Through its mentoring program, Habitat volunteers also maintained an ongoing relationship with the homeowners to help them take care of their new homes and keep up on their mortgage payments. Proof that the Habitat philosophy works could be found simply by looking at foreclosure rates. At the time, the national conventional foreclosure rate was about 5 percent. For the thousands of Habitat homes nationwide, it was less than 1 percent!

Yet there continued to be a lot of public misconceptions about the difference between Habitat-sponsored affordable housing and low-income housing. We had already experienced that when neighbors learned about the possibility of Habitat building in their neighborhoods, they often fought to keep "them" (the Habitat homeowners) out.

One day before we started building at Project Dawn, a local reporter went to visit neighbors near the vacant lot. Several local women approached him, and kept him occupied as they described how they felt about Habitat, the Bigelow Company, and the families who would be moving in. "I think it's pretty cool," said a woman named Georgia, who lived across the street. "The only way we're going to change attitudes is to start right at our front door."

Mary, another neighbor, was equally upbeat. "I think it's a great opportunity for some people to get into a home who might not otherwise have a chance," she said. And Elvira, who lived close by, was trying to round up her church's youth group to help with the construction. "I think giving people a hand up rather than a hand-out is the way things should be," she was quoted as saying. The three women continued to supply the reporter with material until he finally had to leave to make his deadline.

The next day, the front page of the local newspaper's headline read, "Neighbors Welcome Habitat Families." Wow! If there was anyone in the neighborhood that didn't agree, they sure didn't have a chance after that story appeared. While we know these women's names, we weren't sure if they ever came to the worksite again. Was their "interception" of the reporter just a coincidence—or a miracle? Do you believe in angels?

At the groundbreaking of Project Dawn, I used the phrase, "Come on in" several times in my opening remarks to the volunteers and families who had gathered. Before we started work,

I stood with my arms outstretched on the concrete slab, saying again, "Come on in; come on in." Florence was videotaping that day and when I played back the tape, I heard her added whisper of joy, "Yes, come on in." Jesus said, "For where two or three are gathered together in My name, I am there in the midst of them" (Matt. 18:20). On days like this, none of us ever doubted His presence.

Florence and I would swing hammers that day, pound nails, and raise walls with each of the families as "their" section went up on the large, continuous slab. These were moments and times that would alter the course of many lives, just like in *It's a Wonderful Life.* We all count, we all matter, and we all can affect each other for change and for good.

A few months later, the four families—the Mendozas, the Paquettes, the Senas, and the Currins—who had worked alongside the volunteers moved into their new Project Dawn homes. Over the years, whenever we see families come to the Habitat office to pay their mortgage or just to visit, we are never disappointed. They always greet Florence and me with sincere smiles of joy or a mix of laughter and tears. It has been an overwhelming experience to receive the rewards of their joy that they continue to share with Florence and me.

From time to time, we also see the only four families that we were allowed to build for in Glendale Heights—the Compra, Ford, Robles, and Aparicio families—as their children continue to grow and thrive. Years later, these homes are as beautiful today as when they were originally built. The fear of the NIMBY supporters—that our families would destroy their neighborhood—is gone. Florence and I always knew it would happen and now, years later, so does everyone else.

Over the years, other houses continued to be built and more families moved in. The Ferrer and Denson families took possession of homes in West Chicago; the Tee and McLaughlin families moved into their Westmont duplex; and the Rudman family settled in Lombard. We saw Sandra Rudman recently at the Habitat office, and she was just as joyful, hardworking, and committed to her children as she was when she moved into her new home in 1996.

Our experience building in Lombard was especially unique for us. We found a vacant lot that was owned by the village in a residential area near a stormwater pond. I immediately called the mayor and arranged to meet with his staff. They knew that Target was building a new store in Lombard and had agreed to sponsor a Habitat home in Lombard. Seizing the opportunity, I asked if the village would donate the lot to Habitat. Village officials agreed, but with one caveat. The lot hadn't been built on because a major water line ran down the middle of the lot and along one side of the pond, so the lot served as a municipal easement.

I stopped by the RJN Group office and talked Al Hollenbeck into assigning an engineer and a surveyor to the project—pro bono. We quickly drew up a set of plans, hired a contractor, and had the water line moved after receiving all necessary inspections and permits—all in a few short months. Several months later at the dedication of the Rudman home, the mayor himself attended to welcome the family to their new home in the Village of Lombard.

Florence and I experienced many other moving, emotional events during our DuPage Habitat years. During our first year, we gathered enough support from all the Chicago-area affiliates to hold an area-wide fundraising event at the Drury Lane Oakbrook entitled, "Call to Community." Millard Fuller was our keynote speaker, and he moved more than 1,000 attendees with his rousing, energetic, and inspiring words.

Over the next two years, we held annual celebration and recognition dinners with inspirational keynote speakers like

Ron Sider, author of *Christianity Today*, and Tony Campolo, author of books including *You Can Make a Difference*. For me, heroes like Millard, Ron, and Tony exemplify a higher level of consciousness that all of us are invited to reach. It is finding meaning and purpose in giving to others as we have been given to, and being rewarded beyond our expectations.

By this time, Florence and I were into our fourth year with DuPage Habitat for Humanity. Because of Habitat's great reputation and structured assistance, we were able to build the affiliate at a fast enough pace that would allow us to move on to the next part of our journey, whatever that might be. That year Habitat conducted a lot of fundraising to underwrite the Oak Street community, where six families—including the Velas—would move into their new homes.

Yet both of us began to feel that the time to move on was approaching. Earlier that year, I had had the encounter with the hitchhiker and we were still questioning what his words might mean. On a vacation to Florida that April, we'd discovered a community in need, and were wondering if we might be called to pursue our give-back work there. We weren't sure what was next, but it seemed like our DuPage County Habitat work was coming to an end.

Florence and I had made arrangements with the board of directors of DuPage Habitat to hire an executive director, Sheila Frett-Maronta. This was the first time that position would be a paid one. In the meantime, the board elected Chet Staples as the new president. Chet often complimented me on my work and make me feel like he would not be able to fill my shoes. But in fact, Chet was not only a bigger guy than me but would go on to more than fill my shoes with grace and style.

Near the end of our fourth year, Florence and I were honored by Sheila and Chet, the staff, board of directors, volunteers, and Habitat families with a special dinner where we were presented with mementos and gifts. The plaque they gave me still hangs on one wall of my conference room at the RJN Foundation offices.

I had been asked to speak at that dinner, but I hadn't prepared a speech the way I normally would. Instead, the thought of sharing the experience with the hitchhiker six months earlier kept filling my head. I couldn't think of anything else. I had told Florence and only Florence about the stranger and what he said. I had never told anyone else about it for fear of them thinking that I had lost my mind.

I took the podium, thanked everyone, and began to recall the event with the stranger. Without even thinking about it, the words flowed from me as I told them of the hitchhiker that I normally would have never picked up, and how he had been looking for a Catholic church in Wheaton. I told the rapt audience that he had said that God would be calling on us soon to do something very special—and that I had then seen a fleeting glimpse of him one last time, singing in the rain with an umbrella twirling on his shoulder.

As my words trailed off, I feared that the only reaction would be eerie silence. The crowd was anything but silent, however—they gave me a rousing, standing ovation. Their response gave me hope. I might not know what lay ahead for Florence and me, but I knew I wasn't crazy after all.

PART II
LATER YEARS

Chapter Six

HOW DO YOU GET TO IMMOKALEE?

THE FIRST WEEK OF April 1998 found Florence and me at a timeshare at the South Seas Resort on Captiva Island, Florida, near Sanibel and Fort Myers. We'd planned to rest, relax, and talk about where we'd come on our journey so far—and where we might be going. Florence and I had been together for five years, living, loving, and working to make a difference for twenty families by launching Habitat for Humanity in DuPage County. We'd also worked with the RJN Foundation to help many others in need.

In the meantime, my former company, RJN Group, Inc. was having some growing pains, but doing well under the tenacious leadership of Al Hollenbeck and the other principals. I met Al for lunch periodically to talk about the company, and continue to do so today. It has been a heartwarming experience for me to see RJN Group flourish and grow, and to be welcomed back for parties and annual meetings in addition to my lunches with Al.

Before I sold the company, some naysayers felt that the company would never survive without me, but I didn't believe it was necessary to have me at the helm. A company like RJN that paid attention to details with its "We'll Find a Way" attitude towards its clients would survive, with or without me. And as a civil engineer, at heart I was a builder. As such, when the building was done . . . it was time to move on. I hoped that what I had built would be lasting, sustainable, and would improve the quality of life for those touched by my work—and the employees at RJN Group were making that happen. Even today, I continue to be grateful for their efforts.

At Captiva Island, Florence and I enjoyed the temperate, sunny weather and tropical surroundings. We also had a number of unexpected, moving encounters with different kinds of wildlife. One morning sitting on the beach, a monarch butterfly flew over to sit on the strap of her bathing suit, and walked up and down her back for a good fifteen minutes, sometimes stopping to perch on her shoulder. We also saw beautiful yellow and black zebra butterflies, American white pelicans roosting in the trees, and great blue herons and snowy egrets dotting the shoreline. When we kayaked in the shallow waters of the mangroves, groups of dolphins frolicked around us. I believed these beautiful creatures were attracted to Florence, and began pointing them out to her. Florence had come into my life unexpectedly, attracting and amazing me with her beauty. These creatures did the same. If I could have added a new word to *Webster's Dictionary,* the entry would read:

florence (flôr'ens) n. *an unexpected, beautiful wildlife encounter*

We also enjoyed "shelling" together, quietly walking the beach to look for unusual shells. This peaceful activity helped me listen for the voice that was calling me and silence the static rustling in my head. Shelling became a spiritual time for me, as well as a way to appreciate the diversity and beauty of our beach finds. Every time we went to the beach, Florence and I would compare our finds, teasing each other about who had found the most impressive shells.

On Captiva, we witnessed both sunrises and sunsets. Standing on the beach watching the sun recede into the horizon over the Gulf of Mexico, we sang *Amazing Grace* hand in hand. I wondered what the next part of our journey would be, and I didn't have long to wait.

On Saturday night, we had dinner at a local restaurant and danced to Danny Morgan and his wonderful Caribbean music. Florence and I had danced together when we met at Helpmates, and have been dancing ever since. That night, we noticed another couple enjoying their dancing as much as we did. They were attractive and slightly older than us; he was tall and lanky while she was petite. "Doesn't he remind you of Millard Fuller?" I said to Florence, and she laughed and agreed.

The next morning, Florence and I attended church at the quaint, intimate church on Captiva called Chapel by the Sea. As the small interior of this historic white frame cottage-type chapel filled quickly, volunteers were arranging folding chairs outside and placing hymnals on each chair. As we took a seat, we saw the couple we'd seen dancing the night before. After the service, Florence and I approached them, and said that we couldn't help but notice his resemblance to Millard Fuller.

He laughed and said he had been told that before, and that he was a big fan of Habitat. They introduced themselves as Dick and Doris Miller. Originally from Indiana, Dick and Doris were volunteering with Chapel by the Sea to raise money to sponsor and build a Habitat home for the local affiliate in Lee County, Florida. We shared our Habitat experience, and joined them for lunch that day. It was the beginning of a strong friendship. Years later, when Dick passed on, he was buried in the small historic cemetery adjacent to Chapel by the Sea, the church that had meant so much to both Dick and Doris.

At dinner that night Florence and I talked about turning over DuPage Habitat for Humanity to new leadership. We both felt we had accomplished our goal to start and grow the organization to a level that it could continue on without us. As a "builder," I felt it was time to move on, and Florence felt so, too. We had hired Sheila Frett-Maronta, who would take over as executive director while Chet Staples would become the next board president. The board bylaws called for a change after three years and both Florence and I had served our terms on the board of directors. So we agreed it was time. We felt positive both about the state of the affiliate and the good hands we left it in.

But where were we going? Florence and I had talked more about my encounter with the hitchhiker in Wheaton. The first time I'd told her the story, she listened silently, tears in her eyes. She told me later that while she didn't know what the hitchhiker was referring to, she wasn't afraid. From the first time we met, Florence had seen me as a "can do" guy, and she and I believed that whatever lay ahead, we could rise to the challenge—together.

In the Fort Myers Sunday paper, we'd been taken aback by a story about a hunger strike by several tomato farm workers in a town not too far away called Immokalee. Immokalee was in Collier County, near the eastern edge of Lee County, about thirty miles from where we were staying. That article provoked a number of questions, and we wanted the answers to at least one of them—how *do* you get to Immokalee?

The next day we decided to find out. We knew a little bit about the Habitat affiliate in Lee County. A few days earlier, we'd visited the affiliate, met some of the volunteers, and drove through Dunbar, a local community, to see one of the homes being built by volunteers from Chapel by the Sea. Coincidentally, the affiliate for Collier County happened to be headquartered in Immokalee. Or was it another miracle?

As we left Sanibel, and then Fort Myers, we drove the thirty miles straight east on a two-lane road toward Immokalee. While the landscape was flat, we were actually driving uphill as Sanibel is five feet above sea level and Immokalee, the highest point in the area, is forty feet above sea level. Hurricane evacuation signs pointed the very well-to-do from the coastal areas of Naples and Fort Myers toward the east, toward a not very-well-to-do place called Immokalee.

Expansive orange groves lined both sides of the road and we could smell the sweet, floral aroma emanating from the orange blossoms on the trees. Open semi-trailer trucks were parked at intervals along the roads, partially filled with ripe oranges. This area is the heartland that produces most of our juice oranges; the oranges we saw were Valencia oranges being harvested for companies like Tropicana. While the trees were filled with small white blossoms they also contained fully grown, bright, ripe oranges ready for picking.

Valencia orange trees are unique in that their growing season is about fifteen months; trees blossom and carry ripe oranges at the same time, so that the current year's and next year's crops overlap. Because of this, these oranges cannot be mechanically harvested by trunk-shaking machines but must be individually picked by local farm workers, one orange at a time.

Route 82 dead-ends at Route 29 a few miles north of Immokalee, and we drove south into the northern section of Immokalee, which had a few banks and churches with well-manicured lawns. We drove past the middle school to look for the Habitat office. The single-family homes were modest and generally well-kept with front yards of mowed grass and some palm trees, but we noticed a definite lack of sidewalks.

Immokalee lies inland in northern Collier County; Collier County also includes Naples, which is located in the southwest corner of the county on the coast of the Gulf of Mexico. The median income of Collier County is about $60,000 per year per household, fairly close to DuPage County, Illinois. The difference between the two, we would learn, is that while DuPage County poverty is scattered throughout the area in substandard apartment complexes, Collier County poverty is almost entirely concentrated in Immokalee. Immokalee's population of 20,000 residents swells to 40,000 seasonal residents each year. The increase isn't due to "snowbirds" from the North; it is because of the migrant farm workers employed during the harvest season to pick tomatoes and oranges to be sold throughout the United States.

The median income in Collier County was also misleading in that the average income for Naples was about $125,000 per year, made up of mostly passive investment income. Yet in Immokalee, the average farm worker earned about $12,000 per year. This overwhelming disparity results in the $60,000 per year median income for Collier County, which by itself sounds pretty good—even if misleading. Basically it is a half-truth, or as the Yiddish proverb would say, "A half-truth is another name for a whole lie."

The Habitat office building was about twice the size of the traditional ranch homes that dotted the neighborhood. The neighborhood appeared to be lower-middle-class, with some well-kept homes interspersed with others that were run-down. We met one of the volunteers and board members, Thelma Wolgemuth. Thelma, a fragile-looking but attractive woman with a gracious smile, had been a grade school teacher in Immokalee for forty years. This was her life. These were the people she gave it to. Thelma was an active member of Habitat as well as other local not-for-profit organizations. Formerly from Pennsylvania, she was a Mennonite grounded in principles that Florence and I agreed with. Thelma would become a good friend and confidante until she retired several years later to return to her early home and family in Pennsylvania.

Thelma spent six hours with us that day, taking us through town and introducing us to a variety of people. As we toured the poorest parts of Immokalee, we were overcome by the conditions we saw. Sections of town were similar to what we had experienced in Barahona in the Dominican Republic. We had to keep telling ourselves that this was not the Third World, but the USA. We were in one of the richest counties in America, Collier County.

What was going on? Why was there so much poverty? Why were many of the homes, trailers, and shacks in disrepair beyond description? Why were those places allowed to be occupied? Where were the county and state governments? What about the political officials? There were unpaved and partially paved roads, almost no curbs and sidewalks, and open drainage ditches deep and wide enough to swallow a car. We saw conditions that were unsafe, deplorable, and downright scary.

This was a place that had been forgotten by America. A place that had been denied by America. As we saw the worst of Immokalee, we were speechless to respond. I thought, "Was *this* the place the hitchhiker was directing us to go?" But what could we do?

We couldn't fix this anymore than we could have ended poverty in Barahona, Dominican Republic. But we hadn't gone to Barahona to end poverty. We went to contribute to changing people's lives one family at a time. With that experience and the others Florence and I had during our first five years of marriage, could we make a difference in a place called Immokalee?

Thelma made a few stops, greeting Hispanic and Haitian folks at a restaurant, sharing hugs and smiles, and introducing us. Then we'd move on. Her total acceptance of and by the local people was witness to her never-questioning commitment.

Later we realized she was introducing us around so we would have some credibility when we returned to the people and resources that would help shape the work that the hitchhiker had told us would come. Thelma would also give us the names of many key people that we would need to meet over the next several months.

We had nearly forgotten that one of the reasons we came to visit that day was to learn about the farm worker hunger strike when Thelma pulled in front of an old single-story storefront building. The windows and walls were painted with slogans like "Penny a Pound," "Consciousness + Commitment = Change," and "No More Slavery." Inside, a wall-sized picture depicted the Statue of Liberty holding up a large tomato on top of the torch; another large picture showed a worker carrying a forty-pound bucket of bright red tomatoes on his shoulders. Inside, a conference area housed fraying folding chairs, tables full of literature, and an old television set showing videos of farm workers.

A small office was partially filled with fresh fruit and vegetables for people to share with those who needed them. We met several of the workers participating in the hunger strike, and listened to why better treatment and higher wages for workers was necessary. We also met Greg Asbed and Laura Germino. Both trained as paralegals, they were young, smart, and energetic and had devoted their lives to improving the plight of the farm workers. (In fact, later Laura would agree to serve as one of our first advisors on what was to become Harvest for Humanity, the organization that Florence and I would form.)

A few years earlier, Greg and Laura had founded the Coalition of Immokalee Workers. At the time, they were enlisting the help of former President Carter to intervene with Governor Jeb Bush on behalf of the farm workers. As we had met President Carter briefly during our Americus, Georgia trip, we agreed to write former President Carter asking for his assistance with the Coalition.

That day had started as a simple day trip. But it was the beginning of our new work together. Florence and I would have many months of networking, meetings, interviews, and visits, not only to learn about Immokalee but about what we could do with our resources to help bring about some of the needed changes that Immokalee had been waiting for.

Immokalee was suffering not only from a lack of infrastructure, but in opportunities in three critical areas—wages, housing, and education. There was no entertainment in Immokalee, not even a movie theater, and only one drugstore and one supermarket. Most of the jobs were minimum-wage service or agriculture jobs. There were no subdivisions and no neighborhoods for the poor that appeared to be safe and secure. There were no higher education opportunities in Immokalee, and only a handful of students went to college. Students who remained at home had to drive at least an hour each way to either Fort Myers or Naples for any college courses offered by an accredited institution.

The more we learned, the more we realized what was needed was a major paradigm shift. We needed to change what people thought could be done in Immokalee. It didn't take long for us to discover that no amount of meetings, discussions, or conversations would bring about the needed changes without deciding what we needed to accomplish. Although the local affiliate for Habitat was already building homes in Immokalee, the community still suffered from poor wages, lack of access to affordable home ownership, and lack of opportunities for higher education. What kinds of real "brick and mortar" projects could address these issues? We didn't know the answer yet, but for me, this was an example of "We'll find a way" all over again.

While this was the late 90s, wages had not changed for farm workers for many years. Tomato pickers were paid by the bucket and had to pick 300 pounds per hour to earn minimum wage, or just above it. Greg had told me that one of the growers was trying to raise the "bucket wage." I contacted that grower about a month later, congratulating him and his company for trying to make a difference. It gave me hope to know that at least some growers were aware of the wage gap and unhappy about it.

For the moment, however, we were still just a couple from Chicago on a mission from God to collect information to determine what we could do to impact this community. Hopefully, we could at least nudge it in a different direction to improve the quality of life for its people.

That isn't to say that there weren't already people in Immokalee who were already working to make a difference. Thelma had introduced us to Fred Thomas, the executive director of the Collier County Housing Authority. Fred was a stocky, strong, and determined man who took great pride in his work. Over the years the authority had built several hundred modest rental homes with some county subsidy money that provided a relatively safe, secure place for some of the farm workers in Immokalee.

The workers came mostly from Mexico, and while all had documentation, some may have purchased it at one of the flophouses in town. At the time Florence and I did not know why they came, except that they needed work, and the growers needed them to plant and harvest their crops. I learned later that we, US consumers, pay the smallest percentage of our income for fresh fruit and vegetables of any industrialized country in the world. This is an overwhelming statistic when you think about it, but confirms the adage, "When the rich pay the least, the poor make up the difference."

At the time, some believed that growers could afford to pay the workers more but refused. Others believed the price the growers received was so artificially depressed by the actions of box retailers and later because of the effects of NAFTA that only the cheapest labor legally allowable would allow the growers to stay in business. NAFTA, the North American Free Trade Agreement, resulted in more produce being imported from foreign countries. Most of it wasn't grown under the safety and regulatory controls the USDA requires of American-grown food, so it was cheaper. To compete pricewise, American growers are forced to keep labor costs to a minimum, which can result in poor conditions for farm workers.

The more we learned, the more we became convinced that Immokalee was an "upside-down" community. For example, most residential communities average about two-thirds ownership and one-third rental. In Immokalee the opposite is true—two-thirds of housing is rented and only one-third is owner-occupied.

In the 60s and 70s, most migrants came to the area with their families to build a better life and to realize the American dream. By the late 90s, when Florence and I got to Immokalee, this dream was fading and becoming less achievable, if not impossible. Most of the jobs in Immokalee are agricultural-based and most pay the minimum wage. Those wages simply were not keeping up with the cost to live.

The cheap labor force was now being filled by mostly single, unmarried men, who emigrated from Mexico for the sole purpose of finding a job to help keep their families back in Mexico from starving. This exacerbated "upside-down" Immokalee even further as a large percentage of the workers' paychecks were sent back to Mexico instead of being invested in Immokalee. This fact made it even harder to improve local commerce, housing, and education conditions.

But on that first day in Immokalee, our goal was information-gathering. We collected names, phone numbers, thoughts, concerns, and ideas, returning to Wheaton, Illinois a few days later. Over the next two months, as we were transitioning out of DuPage Habitat, we began the work that would shape the future that the hitchhiker had alluded to. What we didn't know was that the day we'd spent with Thelma would impact us for the next ten years of our lives.

When we returned to Wheaton, however, we were surprised by more pressing concerns. The first for me was a fairly routine laparoscopic hernia surgery. While I was nervous about having the procedure, it went so well that I was back in my office the next day. I heard Florence say, a smile in her voice, "what is it going to take to get this guy down?"

The next test, however, would reach into the depths of both of our souls. Florence found a lump in her breast, and called her doctor, who was unable to determine whether it was a benign cyst or a malignant growth. We were both frightened, and wondered if the next step in our give-back journey was about to take a different turn—a much scarier one.

Florence was sent immediately for a mammogram that proved to be inconclusive, and the next day she went to a local hospital for an ultrasound test. During the procedure the ultrasound technician said that she would forward the report to the doctor. That afternoon, Florence went back to her. As the ultrasound test indicated it was a cyst, her physician tried to aspirate it with a needle three times. The doctor was not able to retrieve any liquid and became concerned the lump was more than just a cyst. She referred Florence to a specialist, a breast surgeon, in downtown Chicago.

The appointment was scheduled for two weeks later and it was the longest two weeks of our lives together. In the meantime, we were able to get an appointment in two days with a doctor that was highly recommended by a close friend of ours. He tried to aspirate the cyst but again had no success. The following week and a half we were racked with anxiety and concern. Both of us were worried about what the diagnosis might be, and that Florence would have to undergo surgery.

Finally the day arrived to visit the breast surgeon. After arriving at the specialist's office, we stayed together for moral support when Florence was called from the waiting room to a small examining room. Soon there was a knock at the door and the doctor entered. Dr. Yugiki was in his mid-forties, with pleasant features and a reassuring smile. He greeted both of us and then turned his attention to the reason we were there. We reviewed the procedures that had already taken place.

Dr. Yugiki looked at Florence with great compassion and said, "I know you must feel like a pincushion by now, but may I try to aspirate the cyst before we consider surgery?" Florence agreed without hesitation, hoping to avoid surgery if at all possible. Dr. Yugiki was able to place the needle in the right place on his first attempt and completely aspirate the fluid in the cyst in less than a minute! It was shocking. Florence and I were in a state of total disbelief.

"That was it," said Dr. Yugiki matter-of-factly. "It should not return, and we are done." He asked if we had any other questions and then said good-bye. Florence and I held each other and didn't leave that room for five minutes. We took it as not only the answer to our prayers, but as a sign that we were to go forward with our journey.

Going forward meant continuing to contact the many generous and give-back people that we knew. During our work with DuPage Habitat, we became close friends with a builder with a big heart, Perry Bigelow. At the time, Perry was beginning a new, traditional neighborhood development in Aurora called Hometown. Perry believed that subdivisions lacked a sense of community because garages and vehicles artificially separated people. In traditional neighborhoods like the Chicago I'd grown up in, people congregated, said hello, and enjoyed a sense of community on the sidewalks and front porches. Vehicles were relegated to the back of the homes, in garages and alleys.

Perry was building Hometown to help restore that sense of community in what today are referred to as "TNDs" or Traditional Neighborhood Developments. Through Perry, I came to know several of his friends including Bruno Bottarelli and Nick Ryan, who were building HighPoint Communities in Romeoville. HighPoint was unique in that it was being built with a center where church services would be held and the spirit of community fostered. The spiritual leader, Reverend Dave Ferguson, was one of the original founders of the Community Christian Church in Chicago.

The four men had been meeting every week for a prayer breakfast where they exchanged ideas and fostered their vision for building community. Because of my work with Habitat they asked me to join their breakfast prayer group and I happily accepted. Over the next year, these meetings would help foster my spiritual foundation as well as provide building ideas that would shape the work that Florence and I would do in Immokalee. The breakfast meeting group didn't always agree on everything and we had some heated discussions on—what else—religion and politics. But eventually what took form, after many versions on the back sides of countless napkins, was the layout for the subdivision in Immokalee that would eventually be built.

It was the beginning of the building of my lifelong dream, Bailey Park. What better place to build it than in Immokalee? What better person to help us with that possibility than Fred Thomas, the executive director of the Collier County Housing Authority? I called Fred from Chicago and he agreed to escort Florence and me around Immokalee and share with us his understanding of the "lay of the land" and the powers-that-be. Over the course of many visits in the next two years, Fred would help us obtain recommendations about everything from potential building sites to open-minded bank contacts and approachable Collier County staff members. He was invaluable and we continue to appreciate his friendship today.

In July, we returned to Immokalee and met Denise Blanton, director of the University of Florida Collier County Extension Service. Denise had lived in Immokalee nearly her entire life, and contributed so many ideas that we could barely keep up with them! We were never disappointed in the people that Denise suggested we should bring to the table to help pursue the dream for a better Immokalee. This was the concept that both Fred and Denise had devoted their lives to. Much later, they would express their appreciation for what we were trying to do. At the time, however, I could sense that they both felt we were a bit naïve. They probably wondered how long it would be before this couple, like others before them, would give up on this "pipe dream" and return to the comfortable confines of the Chicago area. During the same trip, we also met Dr. Ed Hanlon, another person who would become important to our work. Ed headed the University of Florida Institute of Food and Agricultural Services (IFAS) facility in Immokalee and would help educate us about farming options in the area.

We knew we wanted to make changes regarding three poverty issues—wages, housing, and education. But we felt that we should tackle wages first as any improvement in opportunities for the people in Immokalee for home ownership and higher education would be closely linked to an improvement in what they would earn.

Unfortunately, the economic conditions in Immokalee were primarily dependent on agriculture in an always-changing economic reality that would be affected by weather, crop diseases, excessive supply or decreased demand, and later, more importantly, by the devastating impact of NAFTA and an unstable labor supply. Every year, new workers come from Mexico to work in agriculture jobs, but after a year of minimum wage, they would often move into better-paying jobs in areas like landscaping, construction, and restaurant service. The next season, growers would have to depend on a new supply of workers, and the cycle continued year after year.

As we talked more with Ed and his researchers, I realized that the economics wouldn't allow us to build a cooperative farm for the farm workers based on a commodity crop like tomatoes. My early analysis of the initial financial investment showed that the quantity of land required was well beyond our ability to finance that large of an operation.

But our early discussions with Ed would introduce us to some other alternatives. IFAS was in the business of experimenting with new crops that would not only be more disease-resistant but that could open up new markets for Florida agriculture that may have been previously untapped. I was swamped with information about crops, soil quality, growing seasons, and potential markets as I also tried to arrange the building blocks of our new enterprise in the right direction.

At the same time, on a somewhat parallel course, Florence and I were exploring what type of housing we might build.

It was time to seek out architects, builders, and engineers. This subject I knew something about, and I was comfortable meeting with them and participating in one of my favorite pastimes—picking their brains. I was happy to share my own ideas as well. However, I think when some of them first heard about our idea of bringing change to Immokalee, they may have wondered if I used up most of my brain cells building my engineering firm.

But others like Denise continued to help. She introduced us to Roy Bonnell, director of the Green Building Project at Florida Gulf Coast University in Fort Myers, Florida. Roy shared his insights, plans, and vision for his green building. Roy introduced us to an architect, Rob Andres, who we talked to about the type of house that we could build in Immokalee. Rob in turn introduced us to Rock Aboujaoude, a very capable engineer working for AIM Engineering in nearby Leigh Acres. All of these people continued to provide us time, ideas, and insights over the next year as our dream began the process of transformation from imagination to reality.

We flew back and forth to Florida nearly once a month that first year to build our relationships with the people who would play key roles as our plans began to take shape. We'd return to Wheaton for several days to visit with our mothers, siblings, and friends. While my sister Barbara was nine years younger than me, we had always been close. She was concerned about our safety and good health, and gave us a lot of emotional encouragement. Barbara didn't always understand the level of our commitment (that was true of a lot of people!) but she could see how important our work was to us. And she and Florence became close friends, and are now as close as loving sisters.

Though we'd just moved into "our" home in Wheaton, we started looking for a house to rent in Florida as well as land that we might purchase to begin the work that we decided to undertake in Immokalee. We also arrived at a name for our commitment. It would be called Harvest for Humanity. I called Millard Fuller, founder of Habitat for Humanity International in Americus, Georgia, to tell him about our plans. He was excited about our dream and its new name.

Harvest for Humanity's mission would be to empower individuals, families, and the surrounding community to help bring about necessary changes and improvements in Immokalee. We hoped to do something new, and develop innovative solutions to the social and economic challenges these low-income families faced.

Florence and I had had doors of opportunities opened for us. Through our work with Habitat for Humanity, we had seen how a hand up, not a hand-out, could open doors for others. Now we hoped to do the same thing for people who, for whatever reason, hadn't had anyone to help open doors of opportunities for them—at least not until Florence and I decided to answer the call of the hitchhiker who we believe directed us to Immokalee.

Chapter Seven

A PLACE TO BUILD—A PLACE TO GROW

THE YEAR 1998 TURNED out to be one of change and transition for Florence and me. We had been inspired first by the hitchhiker and shortly thereafter by our first visit to Immokalee. With the input from our new network of contacts in Immokalee, we began to shape Harvest for Humanity. Our stated mission was to improve the quality of life in Immokalee by developing new opportunities for better wages, homeownership, and higher education. In July 1998, we had our attorney, Alan Garfield, incorporate Harvest for Humanity, as a 501(c)(3) not-for-profit organization—we were now "official."

About a month after our first visit to Immokalee, Florence and I traveled to Habitat for Humanity International headquarters in Americus, Georgia to attend a dinner honoring large donors with the guest of honor former President Jimmy Carter. In addition to helping build a house with other Habitat donors, we met with Millard Fuller, who fully endorsed our plans for our project in Immokalee. "It's going to be difficult, Dick," he told me, "but don't be dissuaded."

Millard even reached out to former President Carter on our behalf. At the banquet dinner with President Carter, Millard tried to persuade him to endorse our new project. The former president was gracious, but later wrote to tell us that while he believed in our vision, he couldn't take on any new projects. We believed that he was besieged with countless requests since he had endorsed Habitat a few years prior, but it meant a lot to me that Millard was willing to ask President Carter to support us.

As we accumulated information and ideas from our Immokalee contacts, we drew up our first white paper and plan for Harvest for Humanity. The next step was to locate land suitable for our project. We first considered a parcel called Arrowhead for our "Planned Unit Development" (PUD). Arrowhead was a 300-acre parcel in the residential urban area of Immokalee, located at the southwest corner of Lake Trafford and Carson Roads. We thought we might use part of the land for a cooperative farm where we would pay farm workers a living wage; the rest of the land would be developed for modest housing at affordable prices. Those houses would be sold not only to the Harvest farm workers, but to other local families already working and renting in the area.

While we were hunting for land, we also met with representatives from the Institute of Food and Agricultural Services (IFAS) to determine what kinds of crops might be viable options for a cooperative farm. Located in Immokalee and part of the University of Florida, IFAS is a research facility on 350 acres that employs thirty-five professors and specialists. IFAS' mission is to improve growing opportunities for Florida agriculture.

While we were initially considering growing tomatoes, we quickly learned that we'd need about ten times more land to make the farm economically viable. IFAS experts including Dr. Ed Hanlon, Dr. Tom Obreza, and Dr. Fritz Roka suggested we consider blueberries instead. While blueberries had never been grown commercially that far south in the United States, they required less land and had the potential for higher profit margins. Blueberries in Immokalee would be harvested during March and April. Chile, one of the major suppliers of blueberries to the United States, finishes its growing season in March, and blueberries in northern Florida and Georgia do not ripen until late April. There would be a small window where we would be able to get a high price for our blueberries.

Ed, Tom, and Fritz helped us evaluate the feasibility of our intended project, and would continue to provide input and help and later agreed to serve on our board of advisors. They received no compensation from Harvest for Humanity for their work while contributing their willingness to participate in our dream.

While a PUD for the Arrowhead property had already been approved by Collier County in the mid-80s, it had never been implemented. One of the difficulties with this location for us was that it was in a residential area. After several discussions, Collier County staffers told us we wouldn't be able to gain approval to build both a farm that required agricultural zoning and a residential housing development on the same site.

The Arrowhead property would not become the location for our ministry in Immokalee. But as we had experienced in the past, one person would touch another, and that person would touch another, and so on. In the future, other people would develop the Arrowhead site to provide badly-needed affordable home ownership opportunities—after they'd seen what could be done through our housing development.

Because of zoning requirements, it appeared unlikely that we would be able to implement our ministry at one site. If we were to pursue the Bailey Park dream, it would have to be at a suitable site within Immokalee while the living-wage farm would have to be at a separate site outside of urban Immokalee. This was a greater challenge than locating and purchasing one site that would be home to both the housing development and farm.

When we were driving past the Arrowhead site, we'd noticed an old, weathered 4x8 foot plywood sign on the property on the northeast corner of the same intersection, diagonally across from Arrowhead. You could barely make out the words "For Sale." When we stopped to take a closer look, we had to walk over to the sign to read the phone number. The sign had obviously been there for years, but was still standing at the corner of a large wooded piece of property.

When we asked about the property, we learned that it had been for sale for at least seven years. The property had been informally designated as "off-limits" by both US and Florida Fish and Wildlife Commission when scrub jay birds had been found foraging in the northeast corner of the property. Because the scrub jay was an endangered species, most people believed the property couldn't be developed. A "kiss of death" label had become attached to the property. Florida's Fish and Wildlife Commission was aggressive about protecting endangered species, and could prevent such land from being developed.

Over the years, the overgrown palmetto fields sprinkled with scrub pines had become an unofficial playground for some of the local inhabitants. The site was carved up with four-wheeler trails, but it was still private property and unofficially designated as a wildlife preserve! It made no sense to Florence and me. We felt compelled to call the barely legible number on the weathered For Sale sign.

We spoke with the property's owner, a retired widow living in Naples. Helen Weinfeld was very pleasant, and listened patiently when I explained our desire to build a Bailey Park in Immokalee. When we met Helen in person, we learned that she and her now-deceased husband had been pioneers in Immokalee for decades. They had built housing and commercial enterprises such as the Immokalee Inn, which remains to this day a nice place to stay.

Helen and her husband had prepared a plan for their own PUD for the 38-acre site which had been approved by Collier County staff ten years prior. They had planned to build an affordable housing development, and had been waiting for final approval from the Collier County Board of County Commissioners. Yet at that meeting, a representative from the Florida Fish and Wildlife Commission announced that the commission had discovered Florida scrub jay birds on the property. As the Florida scrub jay was an endangered species, this finding prevented the board from granting final approval to the PUD project. Such a finding could derail a project, and that is exactly what happened. After Helen's husband passed away, Helen decided she did not have the funds or the help to fight a powerful environmental agency. Her project, for affordable homeownership for local families in need, died.

Before Helen had planned to develop the property, it was valued at seven figures. As word spread that the State of Florida had, for all practical purposes, made the site unbuildable, Helen's dream of affordable housing disappeared—along with the value of her property.

When Helen learned more about our Bailey Park dream, however, she agreed to sell the property for only 25 percent of the original asking price, with a partial charitable donation as Harvest was a registered 501(c)(3) not-for-profit. The sale contract included a contingency that would give us the time to pursue a new agreement with the county regarding the development of the property. Because Immokalee was unincorporated, we always worked with county personnel whose offices were located in the county seat of Naples, one of the richest cities in the state.

When Helen had tried to get approval for her PUD in the past, the State of Florida and Collier County had settled on a division of the property that would set aside the northern 13 acres for scrub jay birds, leaving the southern 25 acres for possible development. When I set up an informal meeting with representatives from the Florida Fish and Wildlife Commission, however, I learned that the state wanted to set aside the entire 38 acres for scrub jays. Yet there was no discussion about remunerating Helen for her land.

This was a bigger issue than I could handle alone, so, I asked our attorneys in Chicago to begin a dialogue with State of Florida officials. Through their work, we obtained an agreement that formally recognized the original division of the property. Rather than fight an unwinnable battle, Florence and I decided to accept the compromise. We could take the next step now—envisioning our new Bailey Park on the site that would become its home. I spent much of the coming months working with our newly-hired local engineering firm, AIM Engineering in Lehigh Acres, and with the architects in charge of the design of the housing development.

Even though we had recently moved into a home of our own in Wheaton in November 1998, Florence and I rented a home in Florida in May 1999 in eastern Fort Myers. Our Florida house was centrally located between Immokalee, the offices of the architects and engineers in Lehigh Acres, and Southwest International Airport in Fort Myers. We began to fly between Wheaton and Immokalee every month—and would do so for the next eight years. Whenever we returned to Wheaton we would work on RJN Foundation projects and visit with family and friends for a few days. Then we would return to Immokalee to spend the balance of the month working on our dream.

When we were in Wheaton, I would attend the Wednesday prayer breakfast meetings with Bruno Bottarelli, Perry Bigelow, Nick Ryan, and Dave Ferguson. We'd discuss the project, and they would continue to modify, shape, and improve the conceptual site plan for the 25-acre housing development. Then I would return to Florida, meet with Rock Aboujaoude, our project manager at AIM Engineering, and present him with a newly modified site layout. I could see that Rock was sometimes torn between agreeing with the changes and figuring out how to go back to his design department with yet one more design modification. In October 1999, I met with my brainstorming friends in Wheaton and had them sign off on a final layout. They all initialed the large napkin and promised to make no more changes. That napkin now is framed and hangs in my office.

The design of the housing site was based on the concept of a Traditional Neighborhood Development (TND). It consisted of forty-nine single-family detached homes and forty condominiums, with plenty of five-foot-wide sidewalks, a park, and children's play areas. Residents would be able to walk to a central location to get their mail, visit the park, play basketball, or swim at the pool. Vehicles would be relegated to the peripheral areas or inside homeowner's garages, which faced an access road at the rear of the homes. The porches and sidewalks all were in the front of the homes, providing a place for children to play and neighbors to congregate.

Although "Bailey Park" was taking shape, I didn't want to name it that. My prayer group in Wheaton had talked about the similarities the plan had with a development in Orlando called Celebration. We were approaching the millennium and the year 2000. The year 2000 would be our "break-ground" year, and in the Catholic Church the year was designated as the year of the Jubilee, where all debts are forgiven and there is a new beginning. As we talked, we came up with the name "Jubilation," and the name stuck. It just seemed right.

The architects and engineers were working hard to finish the architectural drawings and engineering documents so we could seek approval for the project from Collier County. Florence and I had some preliminary meetings with county planning department staff members Barbara Cacchione, Debra Preston, and Ron Nino. While Florence and I had originally been thinking of building twenty homes, their encouragement inspired us to go beyond that number to create a larger development. Barbara, Debra, and Ron all knew that Immokalee needed a safe, secure subdivision that would be a beautiful place for families to live and grow. This was another reason why Jubilation expanded to become an eighty-nine-home ownership development designed to be affordable and available to all local residents.

After presenting our initial documents to county staff in June 1999, the engineering firm prepared the formal PUD documents to be presented to Collier County for approval. Barbara, Ron, and Debra, along with Stan Chrzanowski and Greg Mihalic, assisted us. Their efforts and recommendations to the Collier County board allowed us to move full steam ahead. Without them, the PUD would never have been approved. Their vision for a better Immokalee joined with ours so that the Collier County Board of Commissioners unanimously approved the PUD that paved the way for Jubilation in Immokalee.

But we weren't just focusing on the housing development plans. At the same time, Florence and I were also working on the first reason we came to Immokalee, to build a new agricultural model that would provide "living wages" to its workers. Our dream was to accomplish a paradigm shift in the industry to help pave the way for this needed change.

So Florence and I began searching for another parcel of land suitable for implementing our new farming model. Finding the right property would be no simple task. Denise and Fred, two local leaders in Immokalee, helped run down leads for us. Sometimes we'd visit them to see what recommendations they had. While I sometimes overanalyzed the pros and cons of a specific opportunity, Florence brought added insight to our partnership. She reminded me that we needed to be close to Immokalee, particularly IFAS as we needed its help to grow blueberries, and that we should focus on finding property that was "high and dry" at the highest elevation in the area. We sometimes disagreed, but could always bounce ideas off of each other and fully explore an issue. That kind of synergy helped propel us to achieve what we needed to do much more quickly.

We needed to locate about 40 or 50 acres of suitable land that was close to Immokalee and already zoned for agriculture. We prayed it would not be too far away from that parcel within Immokalee that we had decided on for our housing development.

One morning, Denise mentioned an abandoned orange grove just north of Immokalee a few miles from our proposed housing site. The owner, Clayton McDonald, lived in Arcadia, a few hours' drive northwest of Immokalee. We contacted him and he was cordial and seemed genuinely interested in what we were trying to do.

We arranged to meet him at the property, which was located off of Route 82. We drove onto Edwards Grove Road, a narrow dirt road full of sand-filled holes. The further we drove, the more taken aback we became by both the overgrown terrain along the road and roughness of the ride. "Doesn't this remind you of some of the roads in the Dominican Republic?" I asked Florence. She nodded her head yes, but I think she was really thinking, "Where are you taking me?"

After about a mile, we turned left onto a gravel road toward the property. On our right ran closely-placed rows of mature Valencia orange trees. This was the first time we had been this close to these fully grown magnificent trees filled with both oranges and new blossoms. When we exited the grove, we entered an area that contained dead and dying orange trees. It was obvious that this was a grove that had not been cared for in many years.

An older, tall, stocky man with graying hair was waiting for us. Clayton introduced himself and welcomed us with a strong Southern accent. He had farmed the grove for many years, but a decade before had traveled to Costa Rica to begin a new business and abandoned the grove. The property also contained a partially-enclosed steel pole barn that once housed an office and an apartment but was now completely deteriorated, occupied only by rat snakes and other "varmints."

It was quite a shock for me to think that this is what the hitchhiker had in mind for us. He'd said "many will tell you it can't be done," and looking at the property, I knew our work would be difficult. But, on the bright side, our dream for Harvest for Humanity was beginning to take shape. I could envision converting this abandoned orange grove into a viable blueberry farm even if it would be quite an undertaking. After all, I had no real experience with farming, not to mention no experience with orange trees or blueberry plants.

But Clayton liked what we were trying to do, and said he thought he could offer us an attractive price on the 84-acre site. The property included two existing wells, and did have potential.

I was worried, however, about the thriving 26-acre orange grove that stood between the road and Clayton's property. This property could pose some access issues that would have to be considered before we could purchase Clayton's grove. Clayton told us the grove was owned by Jack Queen, a local contractor and longtime Immokalee resident, but he wasn't sure whether he wanted to sell. In the meantime, I needed more input about what it would take to convert this abandoned grove into a viable blueberry farm.

We met Clayton in early 1999, but it wouldn't be until the end of the year that we agreed to buy the property. While we were spending a lot of our time with experts planning and designing the Jubilation project, I concentrated primarily on the farm part of the project, assisting Florence as she worked on numerous administrative requirements for the housing project. For example, she prepared a comprehensive and exhaustive grant application for the federal government to help finance the housing project. The application was denied, not on the grounds of need (because the need was clear), but because we had not done a similar project in the past. Apparently our project was too risky for the government.

During that year, we also spent a lot of time developing relationships with people who would be integral to Harvest's success. Rock Aboujaoude, our project manager at AIM, became a trusted friend. A dedicated engineer and professional, he was always helpful with suggestions and ideas, and became an essential member of our team.

Our first meeting with Jack Queen, the owner of the orange grove, did not go well. However, we came back to talk with him again and over time, sparked his interest in our project. Yet he told us that he had developed the thriving grove so that he could leave it to his grandchildren. He was unwilling to sell it and we had no alternative but to wait.

That year we got to know some of the people at Barron Collier Companies, a family-based farming business. The company owned much of the property in the area, operated most of the farms, and exercised a lot of influence with the "powers-that-be" in Immokalee. I became friends with Bob Newsome, a Barron Collier agribusiness manager with substantial experience and know-how. He gave me many practical ideas and suggestions, and showed me how to plant and arrange blueberry plants for optimal irrigation, drainage, fertilization, and maintenance. IFAS employees like Tom, Fritz, and Ed as well as Dr. Bob Rouse all gave us time and advice. Tom took us out to his 1-acre patch of blueberries he had successfully developed over the last several years at the IFAS Research Center. The patch was about a mile from Clayton's property, which would turn out to be important for our work in the future.

Jack Queen had told us he planned to save the orange grove for his grandchildren, but a few months after our initial conversation, he decided to sell the orange grove to us after all and focus on a different piece of land for his family. After his initial strong refusal, we saw this as another indication that we were following the path of the hitchhiker.

We were also making good progress with the Collier County Planning Department. Debra, Barb, and Ron began evaluating our early ideas for the housing development and what it might look like on the 38-acre parcel. In the meantime, I continued to analyze the cost to convert the abandoned grove to a blueberry farm. There were many factors to consider including the necessity of building new wells, removing dead trees, leveling the property, and creating the mounds and ditches necessary for the blueberry plants. We'd need a dual-design irrigation system that would have overhead sprinklers to protect the blueberries from a freeze, and a micro-jet system at ground level to simultaneously irrigate and fertilize the blueberry plants. We would also need large quantities of pine bark for planting the blueberry plants.

I also began searching for sources to buy large quantities of potted blueberry plants—there aren't too many of those around. The farm, as laid out, would require 36,000 new blueberry plants, and would be thirty-six times larger than the 1-acre plot at the University of Florida IFAS Research Center. It would be the largest commercial blueberry farm located that far south in the United States.

I focused on the costs, debating if we could afford such a project . . . and if we could wait for the new blueberry plants to mature for the first harvesting . . . and hopefully return our funds. At the same time at the proposed housing site, two miles from the pending farm, we also needed to determine whether we could sell homes at an affordable price that would still return our initial expenditures.

One afternoon while driving around Immokalee, we came upon a new home being built on one of the out-lots in the community. The builder had left some literature about his company at the lot. As there weren't many builders building homes in Immokalee, we called him to set up a meeting. The owner and builder, Jim Boggs, was a young, good-looking, energetic family man with strong religious beliefs. A "give-back" person himself, he identified with us through his own personal experiences and expressed a sincere interest in our project. He told us he would like to participate in a significant way.

This was one of the keys to the project that we'd been hoping for. First, we asked Jim whether he could rehabilitate the old steel barn on Clayton's property. We met him at the farm and explained our plans to renovate the barn including Florence's ideas to build a combination conference/lunchroom room with kitchen facilities as well as a new room for a farm office. Jim not only agreed to take on the project, but gave us a good price to do so.

Things were falling into place for us, but the cost to launch the projects was very significant. Florence and I pondered and prayed about the hitchhiker's message. The project would put much of our life savings at risk. Was this what God wanted us to pursue?

One of Florence's major concerns was that we were looking at not one, but two large and somewhat distinct projects—first, what would be a 110-acre farm and second, a 38-acre housing development. Each was a multi-million dollar project on its own, and the monetary risk would be substantial. Except for the 26-acre established orange grove, everything else would have to be built from scratch. Were we ready to tackle such an endeavor?

We spent many days discussing what it would take and what we would want each project to look like. Florence was always more comfortable getting the farm going first. She felt our calling was to address the wage issues in Immokalee by creating better-paying jobs. If we could build a model farm that paid "living wages," it would make a dent in poverty in Immokalee and would also provide a model for others. Paying better wages was critical to why we were there but to accomplish that with a niche crop like blueberries, never before commercially grown that far south in Florida, would be risky.

Still, based on that vision, Florence and I carved out our mission—one that would address the quality of life for local farm worker residents. The farm would be a place to earn decent wages, learn English, be treated with dignity, develop skills in blueberry farming, and provide hope for the future for the workers and their families. While we still had doubts, as our plan took shape, we believed we could meet these objectives.

As 1999 flew by, we moved closer to launching Harvest for Humanity on a full-time basis. We provided slide presentations of our ideas to several agencies and schools, including Florida Gulf Cost University and the local United States Department of Agriculture (USDA) staff. Dr. Tony Polizos, head of the USDA's soils division in Immokalee, would later help us obtain small grants to help the farm, and remains an ardent supporter of our work today. We continued to keep IFAS and other University of Florida staffers involved to obtain further input and suggestions.

We networked with as many people as we could because we knew we needed to obtain support from local folks like Denise and Fred. Over time, we brought more people on board. The consensus was that the work would be difficult, but that our plan had merit, made economic sense, and could be achieved with the right mix of funds, talent, and hard work.

As 1999 was drawing to a close Florence and I reached a decision, as partners in love and work, that we would donate our personal funds to Harvest for Humanity to purchase the 84 acres of abandoned orange grove from Clayton, the 26 acres of established Valencia orange grove from Jack Queen, and the 38-acre parcel owned by Helen within Immokalee for the Jubilation housing development. Purchase of the Jubilation site was contingent on receiving approval of the Planned Unit Development. In November 1999, the Board of Commissioners of Collier County gave their unanimous approval for the Harvest for Humanity PUD and we closed on all three properties.

Before Clayton and his wife left on a trip to Costa Rica I received a letter that moved me and confirmed that we were on the right path. Clayton hadn't seen the sale of his land as a simple business deal; rather, he believed in and supported our mission. I still have his letter today:

November 1, 1999

Dear Dick and Florence,

> *. . . I wish you nothing but luck and success for this venture you are undertaking. I was very happy to see that the Lord is included in this project, as I feel that the Lord needs to be included in any undertaking that we may have. My wife Mae and I are looking forward to your success and to also enjoying the blueberries that you will produce. We will be praying for you.*

Sincerely,

Clayton and Mae

We were entering a new millennium with the properties and approvals we needed to implement the project that the hitchhiker talked about. This was truly a joyous time. So on December 31, 1999, at South Seas Resort on Captiva Island, with our good friends Dick and Doris Miller, we celebrated and shared our anticipation of the journey ahead.

The night of the millennium party, Florence wore a stunning red sequined dress. As we walked through the crowd, some were captivated by her beauty—as was I. One woman pulled me aside, nodding at Florence. "You are a fortunate man," she said. I couldn't have agreed more, as I looked at the glow in Florence's eyes and her loving smile. As we celebrated the millennium, we gave thanks for what we had experienced already and anticipated the next steps of our extraordinary journey.

Chapter Eight

NO MORE HARVEST
OF SHAME

LATE IN 1999, A reporter and photographer from the *Naples Daily News* came out to do a story on our plans for Harvest for Humanity and our hope for its impact on Immokalee and beyond. Florence and I took them out to the farm—at the time, an abandoned orange grove of mostly dead trees and weeds—and they took photographs of us. We told them about how we intended to transform it from a forgotten plot of land into a plush field of blueberry bushes. A photograph of us ran on the front page of the Sunday newspaper. Florence was in the field, kneeling on one knee, with me standing behind her as we looked out on our literal "field of dreams."

We were thrilled about the article. After all, our purpose in Immokalee was not only to improve the quality of life for as many as we could, but to also raise the level of consciousness of others about the poverty conditions that exist in our country, using Immokalee as one example. We would also ask the agricultural community as a whole why these poverty conditions existed. These conditions were similar to those we'd seen in Barahona, Dominican Republic, and those reported on by Edward R. Murrow in his famous CBS broadcast entitled *Harvest of Shame* that ran on Thanksgiving Day 1960. Murrow's portrait of the plight of millions of migrant farm workers in the United States shocked the country and led to new laws designed to help protect workers from being exploited. Less than forty years later, however, the conditions weren't much improved.

One of our initial tasks was to gather the experts who we had networked with and ask them to serve on a board of advisors for Harvest for Humanity. We had twelve members on our board of advisors as well as a five-member board of directors which met once a year. The board of advisors was more active, meeting monthly at first, and then quarterly. We will always be grateful to the many people who agreed to serve and provide us with the guidance we needed, especially during our first challenging three years as we launched the blueberry farm.

Next, we needed to extrapolate the success that IFAS had had growing blueberries in this tropical climate. Armed with the knowledge from IFAS, personal financial resources, and our spiritual partnership, we set out to prepare the land for what would be the eventual planting of 50,000 new blueberry bushes. The promised revenue produced by this niche crop would allow us to raise wages from $5.15 per hour, the minimum wage at the time, to at least $8.50 per hour and above for farm employees.

We hired subcontractors like Jim Boggs, president of Cypress Construction from nearby Lehigh Acres, to completely gut the existing farm building and convert it to a pleasant meeting place with offices and kitchen facilities. As Jim and his crew went to work on the building, local contractor Jack Queen and his employees bulldozed and burned dead trees, turned over land, and laser-leveled 84 acres to prepare the land for the raised beds and rim ditches our blueberry plants would require.

The new blueberry bushes were only eighteen inches high, but we hoped to see them flourish to six feet and above like those we had seen at blueberry farms in northern Florida. As the fields were being prepared for the first planting, we began to look for office space to open the new headquarters for Harvest for Humanity in Immokalee. We rented space in a new office built and owned by Arturo and Maribel Nunez, who ran a local insurance business. They were a hardworking, dedicated couple who made great landlords—they were kind and supportive and we enjoyed the three years we spent as their tenants.

Once we had office space, we hired Elizabeth DeLaRosa, who became Florence's administrative assistant as well as René Hernandez, who worked mostly for me as our new farm manager. René had experience in farming and helped me to organize the work on the farm and locate and hire the new personnel we needed to start planting the blueberry bushes in June 2000. We also had two key assistants who would work for Liz and René, and they were Carmelita Lopez and Steve Perez, respectively. Years later when Liz and René moved on, Carmelita and Steve would step into their shoes and work with Florence and me until 2007.

That first year on the farm was incredibly busy. Florence's magic touch helped transform the dilapidated old barn into a beautiful conference/lunchroom and office. Eighty-four acres of the old orange grove were cleared, and René and his newly-hired workers planted 12,000 young, promising blueberry bushes on half of the land. Over the next two years, they would plant a total of 50,000 plants. In the other half, he and his workers planted row crops like jalapeño peppers and eggplant that would be ready for harvesting in early 2001. That anticipated initial harvest represented the farm's first source of income. In 2000, the effort and cost was all outgoing—or, as we called it, an investment in the future.

The prior year, Florence and I had celebrated the millennium, full of hope and excitement about Harvest's future. This year's New Year's Eve, December 31, 2000, would turn out quite differently. Once again, we were ringing in the New Year at a restaurant on Sanibel with our good friends Dick and Doris. As we brought them up to date on the farm's progress, waiters brought over several trays filled with a variety of appetizers. After sampling several, I began to sneeze repeatedly. I retreated to the men's room but continued to sneeze. After composing myself somewhat, I returned to the table.

Everyone said I looked terrible, so we excused ourselves and drove to a nearby store in search of Benadryl. Even with the medicine, though, my condition worsened. I became congested like I never had before; it felt like my entire head was filling up with fluid. Even so, I noticed it was getting very cold outside, with the temperature heading toward the freezing mark.

Worried, Florence drove me to the nearest hospital's emergency room. After a short wait, I was admitted into a treatment room. As the hands on the emergency room's clock crept past midnight, we kissed "Happy New Year." I spent the next five hours being treated with injections and oral medications to counteract an apparent reaction to a food I'd consumed. Finally, about 5:00 A.M., the doctor released me with additional medication and orders to return if my symptoms worsened.

With puffy eyes, I managed a few hours of sleep. As soon as we awoke, we drove to the farm to check on the blueberry plants and row crops. The blueberry plants were fine; however, the freeze delivered the second of the "one-two punch" that New Year's Day, as the lush 36 acres of row crops had been transformed by the freeze to frost-covered brown fields laced with dead plants.

Neither of us even spoke at first. We were in shock. Tens of thousands of dollars of row crops were lost. This would be our first, but not our last experience with the perils of being a produce grower in Florida.

Based on the going prices for some of the vegetables, we decided to replace the dead plants with new seedlings—after all, we'd already invested the money to put down plastic and chemicals to grow them. Later in 2001, however, when we harvested the peppers we were forced to sell them below the price we were given a few months back. The price had dropped between the time we planted and the time we harvested, which resulted in a loss of several hundred thousand dollars. We also discovered that if we would have paid the workers $5.15 per hour instead of $8.50 per hour, the living wage at the time, we would have made a slight profit on the row crops instead of taking a significant loss.

In the interim the market price had dropped due to additional competition from foreign suppliers due to agreements like NAFTA. Lowered prices meant that small growers couldn't pay more for labor and stay in business, forcing them to pay minimum wage. If a fair price was contracted between a grower and a buyer ahead of time, however, the grower could pay a decent living wage and still make a fair profit. This fair price could result in a higher price to the consumer, which meant consumers would have to be educated about why they should pay a fair price for "Fair Food." Otherwise there would be no reason to pay more for their produce.

Encountering this experience firsthand led us in a new direction. We realized that not only was Immokalee an upside-down community with regards to home ownership, it was also a victim of an upside-down industry where the grower becomes not the price-maker but the price-taker. We decided early on that there was no way we could sit down with growers and ask them to pay a living wage when all of the risk associated with growing the produce was on their shoulders. Any model designed to help eliminate the problem of poverty in agriculture would have to spread the risk to other entities—namely the consumer and the government—while providing appropriate regulation of brokers and retailers.

Early in 2001, we met with our board of advisors and representatives of IFAS to carve out a new plan to benefit farm workers. The plan would consist of two important facets: first, an introduction of a new label that would read, "Grown and Picked in the USA by Workers Paid a Living Wage"; and second, developing a partnership with the government to provide economic relief to growers that paid a living wage in the form of a tax credit.

We designed a red, white, and blue label that would later be endorsed by Fair Food America. Fair Food America was a relatively new movement that introduced the concept of differentiating US-grown produce where workers are paid a fair wage and growers are paid a fair price for "commodity" produce. Similar to labeling foods "organic" or "organically grown," a Fair Food label helps consumers make an informed, environmentally-friendly, socially-responsible choice at their local stores. Some people have said that "Fair Food" is to American produce what "Fair Trade" is to the world as a whole.

In addition to designing a Fair Food label, we initiated talks with the staff of Florida Senator Bob Graham in his office in Washington, DC. In August 2001, Florence and I flew to Washington DC to start drafting a new legislative bill that would allow growers to pay workers $8.50 an hour while receiving a tax credit of $3.00 an hour; the bill would also let growers become certified as a "Fair Food Grower" and use the differentiating label on their produce.

Doors were closing, so we kept looking for new ones to open. My dad always said that it was okay to get knocked down from time to time—as long as you got back up. The disgrace was to "just lie there," and Florence and I were not about to do that. We were needed in Immokalee for many other reasons; that's why the hitchhiker directed us there.

As we awaited our first blueberry harvest, we continued to build relationships with our employees and the formerly voiceless residents of Immokalee. They could see we were committed to our work no matter how challenging it became. Eventually people began calling us the "Blueberry Couple from Chicago on a Mission from God" (as in the 1980 movie *The Blues Brothers*) after I used the phrase at a church presentation. The name stuck.

We ended up doing things in Immokalee we hadn't expected. In the summer of 2000, a Catholic nun who was also an attorney with the Florida Immigrant Advocacy Center in Immokalee, Sister Maureen Kelleher, came to meet us and ask for our help. There were plans underway to expand the small commercial drag strip at the Immokalee Airport, without providing the necessary noise abatement to protect the low-income residents living nearby. Not only was the drag strip planning to expand, but the Immokalee Airport had big plans to double the length of its runway that would create a flight path over residential Immokalee, our Jubilation project, 1,500-acre Lake Trafford, and the Corkscrew Sanctuary that was home to dozens of native plants and animals. The planned expansion could mean that 747 cargo flights would take off and arrive throughout the day.

This may have been why we were called to Immokalee—to represent the forgotten and the least among us. When a handful of us walked into a town hall meeting one night, we were loudly booed and told to sit down. There were more than 200 people there, all in favor of expanding the track, presumably despite the negative impact on the quality of life in Immokalee. Florence and I were reminded of the terrifying meetings in DuPage County where we'd experienced the fear, distrust, and anger of NIMBY believers.

Fortunately that level of conflict didn't develop at that meeting. Several months later, in fact, people who thought we were against the track expansion came to realize we were really against unabated noise that would be destructive to the low-income families who lived closest to the airport. Although the race track was never expanded, we did come to support it provided that appropriate noise abatement provisions were made part of the expansion plan and that such an expansion would be beneficial to Immokalee as a whole.

Florence and I also attended a meeting of the Board of Directors of the Collier County Airport Authority in August 2000 to argue that the runway expansion could be economically beneficial to Immokalee provided that it was not done at the expense of the residents and the environment. After studying the expansion plan and hiring a noise consultant, we recommended that the plan be modified by turning the expanded runway forty-five degrees from a west-to-east approach instead of lengthening the current runway. As of today, however, the runway has never been expanded.

As the blueberry plants began to mature, I also helped organize the Southwest Agricultural Forum with Florida

Gulf Coast University to develop and address ways to meet the increasing demands of both growers and workers. With the help of Tom Obreza of IFAS, Harvest for Humanity received a grant from SARE (Sustainable Agriculture Research and Education, a USDA program) to test the market for our new Fair Food America label.

During the early years at the farm, Florence and I worked with René, Steve, Antonio, and many of the other employees to improve our growing and harvesting skills. The harvesting season usually fell in March and April while during the rest of the year we pruned plants, irrigated and fertilized, spread herbicide to kill weeds, and treated the soil with sulfuric acid. The naturally alkaline Florida soil wasn't conducive to growing blueberries, so we had to add pine bark mulch and sulfuric acid to lower its pH levels. While we used herbicide, Mother Nature provided us with plenty of ladybugs and assorted pest scavengers so our blueberries were grown pesticide-free. While friends like Gene McAvoy from IFAS and Tony Polizos from USDA helped us determine the best growing practices, the annual cost to keep the blueberry plants in optimal conditions was escalating at an alarming rate.

Florence and I would often share our personal concerns over the economic viability of our work in Immokalee. We'd start every day with a prayer from our daily reader and ask for guidance and the courage to continue our work. And we needed it as our responsibilities continued to mount. As we were working at the Harvest Farm, we also started Jubilation in urban Immokalee, about two miles south of the farm.

Florence and I also believed it was important not only to build a workable model for better wages, but to provide opportunities for advanced education and higher learning as well. We started "Spanish to English" classes at the farm. David Keith, an acquaintance of ours, agreed to teach the classes. He had a master's degree in teaching English as a second language ("ESL"), and offered one-hour classes twice a week to farm workers. We agreed to pay for half of the class time provided the workers stay for the second half during their lunch break. We knew we'd made the right choice when all of our Hispanic-background workers signed up for the classes, excited about the opportunity to learn English.

We began planting blueberry plants in 2000, with the balance planted in 2001. Our first blueberry harvest occurred in the spring of 2002. This harvest was moderate as the plants were still growing but we harvested enough blueberries to distribute to some of the local stores in Naples and Fort Myers. The overall reception by local consumers was good and Florence and I were optimistic about the future. We also planted peppers and other row crops during the fall of 2001. The income from the row crops and our mature Valencia orange grove provided some badly-needed funds to keep us going.

The blueberry plants produced a better harvest in 2003. But it was in 2004 that the plants really took off, and we had such an abundant crop that we were unable to harvest and pack all of the blueberries with the equipment we had. Nonetheless we harvested more than 40,000 pounds of blueberries, and developed a productive relationship with a fruit broker in Plant City. Gary and Chuck helped us as we learned how to pack blueberries in 4.4-ounce plastic containers referred to as "clam shells" because of the way they open and close. Those 4.4-ounce clam shells were then packed twelve at a time into a cardboard "flat," and 220 flats made a pallet for shipping. René and Stephen quickly became proficient at packing the blueberries.

Based on how well the blueberry plants were doing, we decided to hire Jim Boggs and his firm, who had originally remodeled the farm office, to build us a new 80x60 foot refrigerated packing house. The packing house would include multiple air conditioning units, a loading dock for semi-trailers, multiple overhead entrances, and a built-in complete foam-insulated 40x40 foot cooler. We planned to store the packed pallets of blueberries for pickup at the loading dock in the cooler. Jim and his construction crew finished the packing house in time for the 2005 harvest, and Florence and I were proud of our new building.

We anxiously awaited the 2005 harvest, but it came in at about the same quantity as the previous year. We had expected a more abundant crop as the blueberry plants had now reached maturity. Maybe the plants were anticipating what was to come. We broke even, with no real profit. Somewhat concerned, we continued to finance the operation with some financial donations from others, but mainly private donations and loans from Florence and me. In addition, we experienced declining prices for blueberries in the market due to increased competition from foreign growers and consumers wanting to pay less as they became accustomed to cheaper imports as a result of NAFTA.

In late October 2005, Florence and I were back in Wheaton busy with RJN Foundation business when the weather forecast in Florida alerted us to a potential hurricane that appeared to be changing course and heading toward Immokalee. We had believed that Immokalee was somewhat immune to hurricanes as it was so far inland and hadn't experienced serious hurricane damage since Hurricane Donna in September 1960. We anxiously watched the forecasts and stayed in close contact with our employees. I was up most of the night, watching the Weather Channel and tracking the storm on the computer.

Hurricane Wilma originally traveled south of Jamaica and hit Mexico on October 21st. Instead of continuing on its path into Texas, the hurricane suddenly turned east and hit the Florida Coast at Marco Island, traveling directly over Immokalee on October 24th. People in southwest Florida only had a short time to prepare for the storm.

I kept in touch with Steve by cell phone, and our last call was at 5:00 A.M. on Monday, October 24. He told me the wind was blowing so hard that the palm trees were nearly touching the ground. Hurricane Wilma turned into our worst nightmare. It hit Immokalee full-force with wind bands of over 120 m.p.h. that struck our farm directly from the north.

Most of the orange trees had had their early oranges stripped away, which would result in a poor crop the following spring. Nearly all of the 50,000 blueberry plants were uprooted and leveled. Steve was able to hire enough people to work almost day and night to upright and transplant the plants, but the shock was too much. In the ensuing years the plants never returned to their normal production. In 2006, the blueberry harvest was only about one-third of what it had been in 2005, and 2007 and 2008 would be similar.

Our dream of eventually selling the farm to the workers had died. The outstanding loans on the farm now exceeded seven figures even though the land was still valuable as it was located in a development corridor in Immokalee. Expansion and new construction was beginning to move in all directions, and residential growth, highway improvement, and building of new schools in Immokalee was promising. But what would happen to the farm?

Florence and I spent much time praying about our options. One winter morning in 2006 we embraced each other. We'd reached the same difficult conclusion—we would have to sell the farm. (As of this writing the farm is not yet sold, but leased with an option to purchase to a local grower who hadn't been able to own his own land. It remains an income-producing farm with a flourishing orange grove, 72 fully irrigated acres for row crop production, and a productive packinghouse for fruits and vegetables grown both at the farm and elsewhere near Immokalee. However, the land is no longer as valuable. Recently, with the recession of 2008, our farm land has dropped to half of its value prior to Hurricane Wilma.)

Even after leasing the farm, Florence and I have continued to support many of the hardworking families in Immokalee that we have come to love. We have watched in admiration as many of their children are achieving goals that every parent wants for their children. We find comfort with each other in our love and the love we have shared with our extended family in Immokalee. We've become especially close to several of our employees, including Steve Perez. Steve started out as our assistant farm manager from 2001 to 2006, and then took over as farm manager.

Of Mexican descent, Steve was born in Immokalee, and he and I became very close. He's one of the most trusted, reliable employees I've ever had, and the two of us developed a father-son relationship over time that has continued to this day.

Another integral employee, Antonio Ramos, started out as a farm laborer since 2001. He worked his way up to assistant farm manager, supporting a wife and three children. In his early thirties, Antonio is a hard worker who laughs easily and has a huge heart. One of the most satisfying things about the farm has been seeing employees not just work for a paycheck, but have satisfying careers in farming that also let them take care of their families. Antonio and his family became homeowners in Jubilation, and we have enjoyed seeing his children grow.

The first few years, Florence and I celebrated the Christmas holiday with our employees and invited guests with a big lunch meal at the farm. We decorated the barn with multi-colored lights on evergreen wreaths and garland, using a blue ornament, fruit, and vegetable theme. We

invited people from a few churches that were financial supporters, plus people who supported our work like the folks
from the Coalition of Immokalee Workers. Supporters and
farm workers and their families had a chance to eat, talk,
and have fun together.

From 2003 on, we celebrated with our employees and
their families at our home or at local restaurants. One year
the children used a piano keyboard, maracas, and bells to sing
Christmas carols for us. Every year, Florence and I bought a gift
for each child there, and the employees gave us something in
return. Those gifts were a symbol of the love we experienced.

Even in the wake of severe obstacles beyond our control,
we are grateful to have had the farm and the experiences it
brought us. We've also continued to fight for "Fair Food" and
"Country of Origin" labeling. We may not be farmers any longer, but we believe differentiating food as US-grown—healthy
and sustainable—is our best hope for the future, not only for
the farm workers but our country as a whole.

Chapter Nine

THEY SAID IT COULDN'T BE DONE

IN OCTOBER 1999, FLORENCE and I walked hand-in-hand through the 40-acre palmetto field at the intersection of Lake Trafford and Carson Roads in Immokalee. I was about to embark on my lifelong dream—to build my "Bailey Park." I silently prayed that Florence would embrace the dream as well. Although it had always been my desire to build a complete community, we talked about how we had already built individual homes for Habitat for Humanity in DuPage County. We had experienced the enriching feeling of making a difference in the lives of the Habitat families, and we both wanted to continue that kind of work. With our shared Habitat background, my engineering experience, and Florence's accounting know-how, we felt confident that what we envisioned on that field—a new community—could transform lives in a profound way.

A few days later, I stood on an elevated sand mound and spoke to about forty professional visitors from Naples who listened to our plans for a special community on that site. Florence took a photograph of me, arms outstretched, speaking to the crowd from Naples that day. She later had it enlarged and framed for me, and we displayed it in our office for several years. This was one of many ways she showed her support—not only in words but actions. On many mornings she'd also leave "lipstick kisses" for me, setting the tissue she used to blot her lipstick on my pillow. When I returned home in the evening I would find it and the tissue would remind me she'd been thinking of me.

The commitment to undertake a $20 million community building project would undoubtedly test our faith as well as our commitment to each other. Our continuing concern for each other's well-being would help us get through the toughest times and unanticipated obstacles. While undertaking such a large project consisted of implementing hundreds of physical details, the experience was more about the human relationships that developed between us and the many people who would help guide and propel us through the journey. Our networking had helped us create a team of talented local people, all of whom were dedicated and capable in areas including engineering, construction, planning, and law.

Many of the people we met would lead to another introduction of someone who would help us through the next step of the journey. Some might call these experiences coincidences, but Florence and I believed we were being guided by what felt like a force beyond our understanding. We concluded that there was another power at work that would insistently persuade us to investigate what would become new opportunities, each of which helped move the project forward.

While we did have considerable knowledge of accounting and engineering, neither of us had built a $20 million housing development by ourselves—to say nothing of simultaneously developing a 100-acre living wage blueberry farm. Fortunately many other hands would come to the table to guide us on the way.

Rock Aboujaoude, our project manager at AIM Engineering, was one of those hands. He and I enjoyed not only a respectful engineering relationship, but a personal one as well. Florence and I became friends with Rock and his family and shared many meals together. Truly rewarding professional relationships occur when they are based not on monetary success, but on common values—like the belief in sharing resources with others, making decent housing available to everyone, and equal opportunity. Understanding and embracing these values was critical to preparing the necessary plans, specifications, and documents required to build the project, and Rock and many members of his firm, including Paul Pokorny and Joe Lewis, shared these values.

As we began our many meetings with Collier County staff to discuss our plan for this new community, we met Barb Cacchione, principal planner; Ron Nino, manager of the current planning section; and Stan Chrzanowski, engineering manager. All three worked in the Community Development and Environmental Services Division of Collier County. Once again the miracle of our common values came immediately into play as they enthusiastically agreed with the possibility of this new community in Immokalee. They all cared about Immokalee, and suddenly they had an opportunity to help this "Blueberry couple from Chicago on a mission from God" to make a difference.

Barb, Ron, and Stan were immediately excited about the project. We envisioned a new Traditional Neighborhood Development, or TND, for our employees, most of whom already lived in Immokalee. Our new development would include the Harvest Activity Center, a 6,800-square-foot building that would house Harvest's administrative offices, a "welcome area," blueberry store and café, a computer room for community use, a large meeting and banquet area, and a fully-equipped commercial kitchen. The center would be our link to the blueberry farm for visitors from Fort Myers, Naples, and the surrounding areas. Visitors could come for lunch and learn about our living wage, Fair Food, and affordable workforce homeownership models.

Our plan included three distinct neighborhoods: one with forty two-bedroom lower-priced condominiums; a second neighborhood with forty three-bedroom middle-priced single-family homes in a traditional neighborhood design with porches and sidewalks in the front and garages relegated to the rear; and a third neighborhood with nine larger four-bedroom homes. Each neighborhood was within walking distance to the Harvest Activity Center, and the plan included plenty of green space for a junior soccer field, fully equipped playground, swimming pool, paved and lighted basketball court, and additional play areas.

The community would be secure and stable, offer new affordably-priced homes, and be a beautiful, safe place to raise children in Immokalee. It wasn't difficult to convince Collier County staff what we needed to build—and that we needed to build it now.

The county staff encouraged Florence and me to meet with each of the five elected county commissioners one at a time. Each meeting went well; the commissioners were impressed with the descriptive sales literature and brochures we'd developed for Jubilation. With the assistance of Rob Andres, a local architect, we'd completed the design of the single-family homes, the condominium buildings, and the Harvest Center, and the artist's renderings were finished as well. The PUD documents had been finalized for approval, and in November 1999, the Collier County Board of Commissioners enthusiastically approved the project. We closed on the final purchase of the land with Helen Weinfeld the next month, and expressed our heartfelt appreciation for her help. She was thrilled that a project of this type was finally going to be built on the land she'd had such great hopes for.

With Rock's help, we began the search for a general contractor. We met Jerry Wallace, president of the Fort Myers-based firm J.L. Wallace, Inc. Jerry was young and full of enthusiasm for our project and the improvements and opportunities it would bring to Immokalee. Both Florence and I immediately felt comfortable with Jerry and his staff. Jerry had a good reputation, a passion for his work, and was a give-back person. We hired J.L. Wallace, and as we prepared for the groundbreaking day, we also met Dewayne Banks, who would be the project site manager at Jubilation. Dewayne and Jerry had met in the military and had a close and trusting relationship that went beyond just working together. We would develop a similar relationship with both men that often came into play during the course of the project.

This mutual trust helped get us through tough times when numerous change orders and site complications threatened our financial ability to carry out the project. We were able to find a way by making necessary adjustments. One of the major changes came about when I was struggling with the cost and layout of the condo buildings. The approved documents were based on constructing seven condo buildings with eight condos per building for a total of fifty-six units. The buildings were laid out in two rows—four in one row and three in the other, which wasn't very exciting or aesthetically appealing.

One night I had a dream about the layout. The next morning, I greeted Dewayne at the construction trailer and told him I thought we should eliminate two condo buildings—go from seven to five—and turn the two center buildings ninety degrees. This would make a more circular layout with a large open courtyard in the center. The design would also help reduce the costs on the project, although that savings had to be weighed against the loss of sale revenues, with sixteen fewer condo units. It was the right choice at the time as we didn't know how successful the condo sales would be, and Dewayne and our engineers made the necessary revisions to make the design change.

I was trying to get banks to finance the infrastructure but to no avail. Not one area bank was willing to take that risk. After all, nothing of this magnitude had ever been done in Immokalee so few people believed it could be done—and certainly not successfully. While I raced from bank to bank, Florence was busy sending out press releases to local media about Jubilation coming to Immokalee. We printed 5,000 full-color multipage brochures that described what the Jubilation community was all about, and what it would look like when completed. The brochures included artist's renderings and floor plans of the Jubilation homes and condominiums.

Florence and I were encouraged by the inquiries we were receiving about the community. This kept us moving forward even as I struggled to secure financing for the infrastructure. Florence and Elizabeth DeLaRosa, her administrative assistant, kept up with the work at the office as the pace accelerated.

After a lot of discussion, Florence and I made the decision to finance construction of the infrastructure with our own personal funds. We hoped that we would be repaid by proceeds from the sale of the homes.

We broke ground on the project in March 2001. Once the site was cleared, we needed to start installing the infrastructure including underground improvements like sewer, water, and phone lines as well as roads and trees. Many of the utility companies were initially wary, expressing concern about a project of this size in Immokalee. They suggested that we install, for example, water, sewer, and streets for only five or ten homes at a time, "because it would probably take ten years to sell out a project like this in Immokalee." However, we pushed them and they finally agreed to move forward and construct the infrastructure for the entire site at one time.

While networking with bank officers during our first two years, one Immokalee banker said to me, "There have been a lot of folks come to Immokalee with big ideas, but you two are the only ones who have stayed." Local leaders realized what an economic engine Jubilation could be for the whole community. They expressed their faith in us when we received the "Economic Development Award" from the Immokalee Chamber of Commerce, under the leadership of Benny Starling, chamber president, at its annual award and recognition banquet on August 3, 2001. The award read, "To Dick and Florence Nogaj. Thanks for your vision in our community that will provide lasting housing for the citizens of 'My Home,' Immokalee." The award was especially meaningful to us because our project was just starting up. We would often see Benny and his wife, Bernadette, and express our appreciation for their early encouragement.

I was still trying to obtain construction financing for the single-family homes and condos. Once again we were coming up short until a small bank in Fort Myers, Old Florida Bank, led by Larry Johnson took a great leap of faith and agreed to help us. In 2002, Larry secured construction financing for our first condo building and ten single-family homes including two models on the condition that half of them be presold.

Cypress Construction, Inc., owned by Jim Boggs, became the builder of our single-family homes. Jim was a conscientious, give-back person who did whatever was necessary to build the homes. Throughout the project, Florence and I were grateful to be working with people like Jerry, Dewayne, and Jim along with our staff of René, our farm manager, his assistant Steve, and Elizabeth and her assistant, Carmelita.

But now we faced another huge roadblock that threatened the project—the unwillingness of local banks to provide mortgages to our potential homebuyers. Through our work with Habitat for Humanity back in Illinois, Florence and I were familiar with the double mortgages that Habitat used for the financially-strapped families. The families applying for homes in Jubilation faced similar financial conditions—they generally had a little higher income, but were still not able to save for a down payment. They were caught in the cycle of poverty where a large percentage of income went for rental housing, leaving the rest for family needs.

These families also usually lacked financially-able parents or relatives who might provide down payments. After much discussion and prayer, Florence and I decided we would help the families applying for a house in Jubilation, many of whom we were getting to know, with a second "gifted" mortgage that would not have to be repaid if the families remained in their homes for five years.

As more and more families came to our office to apply for homes, we began to build the first two model homes. Florence and her staff worked hard each day helping families apply, unaware of whether they would ever financially qualify to purchase a home. Finding a willing lender was high on our priority list but first the issue of bad credit had to be addressed. Prospective buyers' credit had to be "cleaned up" before most of them could have a chance at mortgage approval.

So we partnered with the University of Florida Extension Service First-Time Homebuyer Program in Naples. For a nominal fee, applicants received a written credit report; an evaluation of the report and detailed direction about how to achieve the necessary credit score; homebuyer educational seminars; mortgage application assistance; and sale contract closing assistance.

In early 2001, First-Time Homebuyer staff came to the Harvest for Humanity office for four hours on a Saturday afternoon to begin the process with about thirty prospective homebuyers who had contacted our sales staff. However, none of the prospective homebuyers ever contacted either the First-Time Homebuyer staff or Harvest staff and no one knew the reason why. After talking with the First-Time Homebuyer staff, we learned that while many of the families met the required minimum of approximately $35,000 in annual income, most of them had monthly debt expenses that exceeded the 41 percent limit to attain mortgage financing. Nearly all had poor or nonexistent credit, and were overwhelmed by the prospect of cleaning it up. Finally, the First-Time Homebuyer Program did not have the personnel resources to work one-on-one with buyers.

We realized that if we were going to sell these houses we would have to actively help prospective buyers become qualified. Florence contacted Credit Data Services, a credit company in Fort Myers, which agreed to collaborate with us. Its staff provided software and taught us how to use it, how to read credit reports, and how to take the steps necessary to clear negative credit. Florence and her staff reviewed hundreds of credit reports to help qualify prospective buyers for homes. We were working to create homebuyers. But who would take a chance on them and loan them the money they needed to purchase their homes?

Once again, an "angel" would come to our rescue. One morning our friend Benny Starling, president of the Immokalee Chamber of Commerce, brought Carol Kirchdorfer, a representative of the Huntington Mortgage Group headquartered in Columbus, Ohio to our office. The timing was right because Huntington was looking for a project like ours that would coincide with its Community Reinvestment Act requirements. (The CRA encourages lenders to provide financing to homebuyers in low- and moderate-income neighborhoods.) Carol immediately went to work gathering data on a few of the prospective buyers to take back to her home office. She was, and has continued to be, encouraging and supportive.

This was a major turning point for us on the project. Eventually, Carol's firm helped finance a majority of the homes in Jubilation. Many others were financed through Florence's efforts to implement the mortgage assistance program by the USDA Rural Development program. Over 3,000 families would eventually visit our Immokalee office to inquire about our homes, over 90 percent of whom were from Immokalee. During those early years, Florence and the staff processed over 1,000 applications. It was clear that the demand for affordable housing was high, and that Jubilation would only start to meet that demand.

Florence and I spent countless evenings at the Home Depot store in Fort Myers looking for ideas and hardware for our model homes. Once again we were decorating a home together—but this time the home wasn't for our personal use but to show prospective Jubilation buyers what to expect. Once the models opened, sales began to increase dramatically. Florence's office assistant Elizabeth turned out to be our first condo buyer, and one of the first buyers of a single-family home was the newly-hired assistant at our office, Carmelita Lopez, and her family.

The models had a dramatic impact on a banker as well. Steve Price, chairman of the board of Florida Community Bank, and his father, the bank's founder, visited the models shortly after they opened. Not long after that, we met with Steve and Ray Holland, president of the bank, and signed a loan agreement for construction financing required for the balance of the homes and condos in Jubilation. What made it significant was that it required no "presales" or sales contracts before we could break ground on any new buildings.

This was another turning point for the project. Before that, it had appeared that Jerry Wallace and his crew would have to amend his contract with an extended schedule. Thanks to financing provided by Florida Community Bank, and with construction contracts no longer in jeopardy, we were able to accelerate the construction of the remaining buildings and the sale of the homes. We'd heard many people in Immokalee say that Jubilation could not be done, that condos would never sell in Immokalee, or that it would take at least ten years to financially qualify eighty-nine buyers for the homes. In reality, it took about eighteen months to sell almost all of the houses and condos, and less than three years to build out 90 percent of the project.

We now turned our attention to the building that would represent all that Florence and I came to do in Immokalee. We wanted to make the Harvest Activity Center a very special place. It was carefully designed to include all the amenities that we hoped would continue at Jubilation after Florence and I moved on. Our plan was that it would provide educational classes utilizing a fully-equipped computer room with twelve new computers purchased with donations from key people in Immokalee. In back of the computer room would be a small children's library that would provide reading opportunities for the younger residents of Jubilation.

The center of the building would contain an expansive welcoming and waiting area with comfortable couches, a large television, and a lounging area equipped with tables and chairs for meetings and casual dining. A fully equipped commercial kitchen would provide healthy lunches to the general public while giving us the opportunity to spread the word about what we were trying to accomplish in Immokalee.

The center would also provide new job opportunities for local residents of Jubilation, not only in the kitchen, but also in the Blueberry Store and Gift Shop and the Harvest for Humanity administrative office area. The Blueberry Store and Gift Shop were designed to attract visitors from Fort Myers, Naples, and the surrounding area to come to Immokalee for special lunches and feast on our homemade blueberry pies and muffins. Visitors would pick blueberries right across the street at our 1-acre blueberry "U-Pick" and enjoy the ambience while hearing about Harvest from Florence, Elizabeth, Carmelita, or me. When Steve and René were not working at the Harvest farm, they would also take time to tell visitors about their work. The message was always about improving the quality of life in Immokalee through new opportunities like the living-wage farm, the affordability of the new homes in Jubilation, and by improving education through computer literacy and learning English at the ESL classes.

We finalized the plans for the Harvest Center with r.j. mccormack architect, inc., our architects from Fort Myers. Once again, J.L. Wallace, Inc. with Dewayne Banks as the site supervisor would construct the building. But before we

Above: Dick working with the crew to help plant the first blueberry plants at Harvest farm.

Below: Stephen Perez, asst. farm manager (far left), with employees packing Harvest blueberries.

Left: René Hernandez, Harvest farm manager, prepares to plant the first 8,000 blueberry bushes.

Below: Label that can be affixed to Fair Food produce grown in the USA.

Above left: Dick at the farm holding the initial "hand-made" Harvest Blueberries label.

Above right: Dick with Jim Boggs, president of Cypress Homes, Inc., who renovated the office at the farm and partnered with us to construct 49 single-family homes at Jubilation.

Above: The Harvest Blueberries label professionally created by graphic designer Pat Shapiro, owner of Flying Colors of Naples, Inc.

Left: David Keith (far left) with Harvest farm workers during one of the ESL classes held at the Harvest farm office.

Above left: With Thelma Wolgemuth, center, who was our first contact in Immokalee and our greatest supporter.

Above right: Dick with Benny Starling, president of the Immokalee Chamber of Commerce and a good friend.

Left: Dick speaking to the Naples Press Club during a "Future of Immokalee" tour in April 2000, just before land clearing.

Below: Dick with Jerry Wallace, president of J.L. Wallace, construction management firm for development of Jubilation.

Jubilation **Coming Soon**
ffordable Garden Home Condos
and Single Family Homes
stom Home Lots Also Available
57-4888   a Harvest Community

Above: The first condo building ready for new residents in August 2002.

Left: Carol Kirchdorfer, Huntington Mortgage Corporation, and a co-worker. Huntington provided many 30-year attainable mortgages.

Below: An aerial photo of the completed 26-acre Jubilation subdivision.

Top: The first five homes completed in Jubilation and ready for homeowners to move in.

Above: The Froylan Resendiz family on home closing day with Elizabeth DeLaRosa (far right).

Above: Resident Max Surin, receiving his family's basket of gifts, was a teenager when his family bought a home in Jubilation. Max will graduate from Michigan State University in 2010.

Left: Francisco and Grisel Gaspar are happy after becoming first time home owners.

Above left: Dick and his sister, Barbara, surveying the "living courts" at Jubilation. Houses face a sidewalk and the garages are in the rear of the homes.

Above right: Perry Bigelow, president of Bigelow Homes, Inc., visited the site he helped lay out.

Above: Our dear friends Dick and Doris Miller are among a group of strong supporters from Captiva Chapel by the Sea Church who attended a holiday lunch at the Harvest farm.

Right: Fred Thomas, retired leader of the Collier County Housing Authority and a long-time Immokalee resident, was there to help us from the beginning and remains a good friend.

Above: A group photo of Jubilation residents attending a homeowner's association meeting in August 2003—one year after families first began moving in.

Below left: Residents Jacob and Carmelita Lopez accepting a basket of gifts upon move in.

Below right: Florence with Jubilation resident Gloria Dominguez.

Above: The Harvest Activity Center, which was donated to Hodges University in 2007.

Right: Carmelita Lopez, recipient of the first Hodges University Dick and Florence Nogaj Scholarship designated for Jubilation residents.

Below: Dick and Florence with Terry McMahon, President, Hodges University, and members of Hodges University Student Ambassadors.

could begin construction, we had to obtain financing for the building that would consist of an initial construction loan that later would be converted to a short-term mortgage requiring a balloon payment at the end of the contract period. I set off to approach several banks in the area. Fifth Third Bank in Naples agreed to help us meet the challenge, in large part due to the bank's president, Colleen Kvetko. She became another angel on our behalf. Once she became familiar with our work, she championed what we were trying to accomplish and was able to secure approval from her board to finance the center with one caveat—a mortgage guarantee from USDA.

Colleen's assistant, Byron Scullin, became a close ally who helped us try to obtain a mortgage guarantee from USDA. Once again, however, because of the uniqueness of the project, USDA refused to issue the guarantee. This should have killed the Harvest Center, but Colleen eventually was able to secure the loan for us without the USDA guarantee. This was another one of those "miracle moments" for Florence and me as we celebrated it with a groundbreaking ceremony with Colleen, Byron, Dewayne, and the Harvest staff. After several years, Harvest for Humanity was going to be moving to a new home.

Construction progressed quickly under Dewayne's supervision as we overcame one obstacle after another. Building code changes required us to add, for example, more electrical outlets, build fire walls for the kitchen, and install panic bars on nearly all the doors. The building had many special features that required additional inspections, and I worried that we would fall behind. But we finished the building on schedule, and moved into our new administrative offices in the summer 2003. Flags announced the fact that our sales office was now located at Jubilation, near our model homes, rather than at an offsite location.

We also began to hire people to staff the kitchen and prepared to open the café and dining room. We ordered most of the cooking and serving equipment, and the Regency Hotel in Naples donated furniture and dishes to us. Florence and I kept "learning on the job" about running a restaurant and a gift shop. Florence and her staff worked long hours getting the necessary certifications and permits to open the kitchen, café, and dining room and be ready for business.

The computer room was being equipped with twelve new stations. With the help of local consultants, the Blueberry Store was taking shape with a computerized cash register; shelving with blueberry-related inventory; and custom-made items such as shirts, aprons, and hats with embroidered Harvest logos.

It was all coming together. The building had plenty of office space, and we even had a sales area with a gallery of artist's renderings on the wall for the homes being built so would-be home buyers could study the pictures before making their decision. In the meantime, we all worked feverishly as the big day approached—November 23, 2003.

Almost 200 people joined us for the Grand Opening for the Harvest Center at Jubilation. Dozens of friends and business partners who had helped make this day possible were present, and it was truly a remarkable experience. The weather was glorious, the ceremony was prayerful, and the message was promising. Although it was a dream come true for Florence and me, we didn't realize our biggest challenges still lay ahead.

Enough of the new homes and condominiums had been completed so that Florence and I could purchase one of the condos and move in that year in May 2003. Our models also had been sold, so Florence was able to furnish our two-bedroom condo with the living and dining room furniture from the condominium model home. We were grateful that we would no longer have to make the fifty-mile round trip from our rental home in Fort Myers to Immokalee every day. Now, Florence and I would have the ability to work more efficiently with our office only 200 feet from our condominium home. We even found time to go to the beach a few Sundays to shell and snorkel together.

After our Grand Opening, we were ready to move forward with a new leap of faith, not knowing exactly what to expect. We were still focused on building out the Jubilation site, selling homes, helping homeowners obtain mortgages, and welcoming them into the community, but opening and operating the Blueberry Store and Harvest Café brought another new element into our life. Running these businesses consumed us more and more.

Florence worked very hard overseeing the Harvest Café with Liz and Carmelita. The three of them trained staff, prepared and served meals each day, catered weddings and parties, and helped keep the kids in the computer room and around the center properly and educationally engaged. Florence also spent a lot of time organizing activities for the local residents and their children that included parties, movie nights, soccer games, martial arts classes, and Weight Watchers meetings.

Florence hoped that she could pass some of the responsibility of organizing these events to some of the Jubilation residents, but this generally didn't happen. With our Jubilation families, we saw some similarities to what we experienced in Barahona, Dominican Republic, as opposed to the experiences we had had with Habitat in DuPage County, Illinois. The largest difference had to do with volunteering.

A great degree of Habitat's success in general is due to the many unpaid hours that are donated by primarily financially well-off volunteers. In Barahona, however, there were no volunteers because there were basically no well-off people who had the time or ability to give of themselves. In Immokalee we discovered a similar situation—few well-off volunteers. Yes, some people would travel from Naples and Fort Myers, but they usually only volunteered for short stints. Without people volunteering, all necessary and optional services had to be paid for.

Part of the problem may also be due to the fact that some of our residents were used to receiving charity rather than volunteering themselves. Over time, though, Florence and I saw Jubilation residents beginning to make the paradigm shift from "what else do you have for me?" to a more empowered position of "what do I have to offer you?"

Throughout 2004 and 2005, Florence and I began to feel a sense of worry that became a grave concern. We didn't know if the dream we had envisioned was going to be sustainable. We were running out of personal funds while government grants mostly went elsewhere. Fortunately, we did set aside enough personal funds to complete Jubilation and we were thankful for the scores of wonderful families who were able to purchase homes and condos.

In August 2005 we joyfully celebrated with Antonio, our assistant farm manager, and his family, the closing on his home—the last sale in Jubilation. Jubilation was nearing completion and despite all of its challenges, could be characterized as a success.

Then in October 2005, Hurricane Wilma brought damage to Jubilation. Although it was minor to the buildings, more than one hundred trees, primarily oaks planted three years earlier in the parkway next to the streets, were uprooted. We asked the owner of Johnny's Loader Business, to help upright the trees. While Johnny was overwhelmed by the needs of his relatives and at his own house due to all the damage in Immokalee, he still agreed to help us. He brought his equipment in and with the help of our employees and the young teens who lived in Jubilation and were organized by Elizabeth and Carmelita, the trees were set upright in two days. All of them survived! Jubilation quickly returned to its original beauty thanks to the efforts of Johnny and everyone else.

Immokalee lost electric service, however, for a week or two. Steve hooked up the three generators we'd purchased in the event of a power outage, and Liz was able to use the Harvest Café kitchen to prepare food and allowed Jubilation residents to cook there also. Many Immokalee residents weren't as fortunate; a great deal of the housing in Immokalee was mobile homes, many of which were damaged. Our employees reached out to those in need. For example, two days after the hurricane, our regular mail carrier arrived on her scheduled route. She told Liz she and her family lived in a mobile home and the roof had caved in, flooding everything inside. Her children were hungry and she had no food at home. Liz didn't hesitate a moment and prepared a pancake breakfast to go for Juanita and her family of four.

While the natural disaster had passed, another storm was brewing—this time, within the homeowners' Jubilation Community Association. All homeowners were automatically members of the association, which had its own board of directors. After the first board, we recruited homeowners with experience in accounting and management, but soon ran into issues we hadn't expected.

One involved the payment of association fees, which were becoming out-of-reach for many families. Association fees pay for the maintenance of all of the common areas of Jubilation and guarantee the upkeep of the entire neighborhood. But many of the Jubilation residents didn't see the association fees as an investment in their home, which wasn't surprising. After all, Jubilation was the first homeowners' association in Immokalee, and while Florence and I explained the structure and rules of an association before, during, and after each home sale, most residents didn't fully comprehend the full extent of what was expected of them as homeowners.

We were confident that those costs would be returned to them in the future if and when they sold their homes at market value. Eventually the board developed a fair fee structure, and the majority of homeowners accepted and learned to appreciate association living. But there were a few trouble-makers. Some tried constantly to "stir the pot" and create problems where there were none. While this may have been expected, it was difficult for me and especially Florence not to take things personally. Although the vocal nay-sayers eventually moved out, they left broken relationships in their wake.

It would take several years for trust to be rebuilt and to recreate a sense of community. Florence and I worked hard behind the scenes to make that transition happen. When we welcomed Tom Carmichael, a new resident to the community, he was glad to step up to serve as president of the Jubilation Community Association. He had experience with previous homeowners' associations and helped steer the board on a promising course for the future.

Even as we overcame this challenge, we continued to experience a series of setbacks at the farm that kept knocking us down, daring us to get back up again. The pressure of trying to keep the blueberry farm intact, and responding to the wants and needs of Jubilation homeowners, proved to be too much for our farm and site manager, René. He had given his best over the six years he worked for us, but he finally resigned, and we hugged good-bye.

We had obtained a grant from Collier County in 2004 to help operate the Blueberry Store and Harvest Café. We began taking it to another level with a more expansive plan to market the products to Naples and Fort Myers. However, when it came time to renew the grant a year later, we were unable to get the grant renewed. Shortly thereafter, Elizabeth left our employ. Carmelita, with Florence's help, was able to step in and keep the office and the Harvest Center on track. Grisel Gaspar, another employee, also stepped up and became an excellent assistant for Carmelita. A resident of Jubilation, Grisel is a petite, good-looking young woman who also happens to be very smart. Grisel is committed to her family, and has a fine husband and two terrific young children. Both Carmelita and Grisel were wonderful ambassadors for Harvest for Humanity.

It was our relationships with the Jubilation homeowners that helped Florence and me weather these tough times. Carmelita was one example of someone we saw grow in many ways through Jubilation. She started out as our office assistant and with her husband and three young sons was one of the first families to move into a home. Carmelita had a great work ethic, and was smart, compassionate, and trustworthy. She "held down the fort" at the office when Florence and I would travel home to Wheaton for about four days each month. Over time, she became surer of herself and her capabilities, and eventually was elected by the other residents at Jubilation to the Association's board of directors. She continued to do a great job at the office and still maintain her passion for her husband and children. Carmelita and her family have become part of ours as well.

Even with the support and love we gave and received, though, dealing with and overcoming obstacles hit us hard. The continuing financial losses at both the farm and the Harvest Activity Center strained our partnership. Now we needed to focus not only on the families we'd helped, but on our own relationship. I couldn't have made this journey without Florence, and I didn't want to lose her. Together, we would find a way— no matter what happened next.

Chapter Ten

THE SEVEN-MINUTE MIRACLE

FLORENCE AND I HAD spent more than seven years working toward our dream of building a Bailey Park and a sustainable farm that paid its workers a living wage in Immokalee. While our work was incredibly rewarding, it was also taking a toll on us. Florence had been hurt by some of the "pot-stirring" homeowners who had now left Jubilation, and I was constantly worried about the financial pressures the farm was facing as well as what the future might bring.

In lighter moments I would sometimes ask Florence, "Well, do you see a light at the end of the tunnel?" She would shake her head. "I'm sorry, Dick, but I do not see that light yet." Her words would jolt me back to reality, and I would realize I needed to get back to the drawing board and figure out what our next step was.

We had to remind ourselves that the hitchhiker did not direct us to Immokalee to lose our way but to do what had not been done before. This was to accomplish three objectives in Immokalee: (1) decent, fair, and living wages; (2) affordable homeownership opportunities; and, (3) higher education opportunities. These goals would not completely transform Immokalee but would use our God-given talents, time, and treasures to impact lives for the better and create an example that we hoped others would be inspired to emulate.

Our relationship was sometimes strained, and we needed to openly evaluate where we were on our journey and avoid unresolved emotional conflicts that could hurt our bond. We fell back on the Imago process we'd learned, using active listening and sincere empathy to maintain our connection. Florence knew how worried I was about the monetary issues and I knew that the emotional issues were putting a heavy strain on her.

A few times Florence returned to Wheaton without me for several days to search for inner courage and strength. Time apart also gave me time to collect my thoughts and ponder our future. When we reunited I would tell her not to worry. We would find a way!

We did know that Jubilation had impacted Immokalee. The community now had a beautiful subdivision with hope inscribed all over its foundation. The homes that had risen from that foundation symbolized what was possible. Parents' and children's lives were permanently improved. Because of Jubilation's success, Arrowhead, a new housing development of several hundred homes sprang up across the street, offering moderately-priced homes for working families.

As Florence and I determined our next step, we made the difficult decision to sell the Harvest Activity Center in early 2006. Although the tourist season was just beginning, we knew it wouldn't generate enough income to meet annual expenses. The Harvest Café was not self-sustaining, and the Blueberry Store had little income in the off-season. We could no longer afford to subsidize the businesses at the Harvest Center.

We hoped to sell the center to one of the not-for-profit agencies in Immokalee that could use it to bring needed services to the community. We talked with many people at different agencies, but the non-profits were mostly interested in discussing donation of the center and none seemed to be in a financial position to purchase it or assist with the remaining mortgage on the building at that time.

Our options were shrinking. If we had to donate the center (as opposed to selling it outright), we wanted it used for higher education, which had been unattainable for Immokalee residents for many reasons. And this was the one primary goal we hadn't accomplished—to bring educational opportunities to the people at Jubilation and the surrounding area.

We discussed this idea with our close friend Jim Kean, who divides his time between Chicago and Naples. When in Florida, he dedicates his time as a volunteer at Guadalupe Social Services in Immokalee working with the poorest of the poor. Jim agreed with us that donating the center to a local college to use as a satellite-learning center was an outstanding idea and suggested International College (IC) as a possibility. IC had main campuses in Naples and Fort Myers and learning sites in nearby communities; in May 2007 it would be renamed Hodges University. IC/Hodges wasn't a "typical" university in that it doesn't have sports teams or dormitories. It targets returning students and recent high-school graduates who are working full- or part-time while attending college.

It sounded like an excellent match, especially as we learned more about the college. Dr. Jan Brock, vice-president of academic affairs, visited us on September 12, 2006. The meeting was positive and exciting, and the next day, Hodges President Dr. Terry McMahon and several other college officials including John White, chief financial officer, toured the facility. After a thought-provoking discussion, they told us they were interested in the possibility of entering into an agreement with us.

The agreement would transfer title of the Harvest Activity Center and the remaining mortgage of approximately half of the building's value to the college to become a learning satellite site for the university in Immokalee. The agreement also included the outright donation of other properties owned by Harvest for Humanity including a twelve-acre Conservation Preserve, a 2-acre parcel across from the center formerly used as a "U-Pick" blueberry field, and a 3,200-square-foot metal storage/maintenance building with 800 square feet of finished, air-conditioned office space.

To say that Florence and I were overjoyed was truly an understatement. Before we started talking with representatives from Hodges, we were convinced that we would have to leave the center vacant and abandoned because of our inability to keep it open. Instead it would now be fully utilized for providing higher education opportunities not only to the residents of Jubilation but the surrounding community.

Florence and I were overwhelmed by the graciousness and positive response from the leaders of Hodges. Terry, the college president, had founded it over twenty years ago and built it into a thriving institution. Terry is a soft-spoken man of faith, equipped with the necessary tenacity to get things done, and he and I quickly "clicked" on many levels. John White, Jan Brock, and Dave Rice, vice-president of information technology and facilities management, all showed the same tenacity as we moved forward with the plan to transfer ownership of the center.

John requested a list of our operating expenses and used the number of possible classrooms and student capacities to determine whether Hodges could efficiently provide educational opportunities at the center site. Jan developed a plan to adapt the building for Hodges' needs. Actually few changes were needed to quickly transform the building into four possible classrooms plus the existing computer room, while the Blueberry Store could be converted into a bookstore. The design of the building would accommodate a quick transition to a college satellite site with little or no structural changes.

We met with Hodge's attorney, Michael Volpe, and reviewed the existing Planned Unit Development (PUD) documents that governed the use of the center. They had been prepared by Florence and me with help from AIM Engineering firm and the planning staff at Collier County and were approved in late 1999. We were grateful that we included in the original PUD "educational classes" as a possible use of the building—after all, we'd anticipated that they would be held someday at the center. Because of this fact, we were confident that a simple letter submittal to the county requesting approval of the existing PUD documents would be forthcoming.

Before we entered into a sales contract, however, we agreed that we should present the idea to the Jubilation Community Association Board of Directors and the Jubilation homeowners. We were met with widespread approval as people welcomed the opportunity to have college classes available in Immokalee. Jubilation residents were also excited and grateful to hear about the scholarship program Florence and I would set up to help them attend classes at Hodges. With the scholarships, any Jubilation resident would receive a $500 grant per student, per semester, with a total of $1,000 per year, as long as he or she maintained a "C" average. (To date, five Jubilation residents have received scholarships.)

The next step in the process was to meet with our Collier County District Five government representative, Jim Coletta, the chairman of the Board of Collier County Commissioners. There were five county commissioners in Collier County, with one commissioner representing each of five districts. Jim had been the district five commissioner for many years, and had been a good friend of Harvest. He worked hard to keep Immokalee "in front of the board," so to speak.

Terry and I visited Jim and presented him with the idea of Hodges establishing a presence in Immokalee at Jubilation and what it could mean to the community. He was elated and all for it, and promised to help try to obtain a quick approval so Hodges could start preparing for the opening of classes as soon as possible.

When it had become apparent that Florence and I would have to find a buyer or donor to take over the Harvest Center, our employee Carmelita had become concerned not only for us but for what might happen to her own job. Carmelita had been with us from the beginning, and was smart, dedicated, and hard-working. We assured her that we would find a way for her to stay on; it seemed logical to have Carmelita stay on and assist with transforming the Harvest Center into a new facility of Hodges. She interviewed with Hodges staff and was assured that after the anticipated closing and transfer of the property, she would be working for them from then on.

The last hurdle in this part of our journey was to obtain what we believed would be routine approval by the county of the transfer of ownership of the center from Harvest to Hodges University. There was no money changing hands and both entities were 501(c)(3) not-for-profit organizations. The existing PUD already listed educational classes at the center as an approved activity at the Harvest Center.

Florence and I looked forward to working with the county on this last leg of the journey. Seven years earlier, working with county staff including Barb Cacchione and Ron Nino had been one of the best experiences I have ever had working with a municipal government. With the cooperation of the county, we had been able to build Jubilation, a safe, secure place for eighty-nine families and over 200 children. So we anticipated that this next step would be a simple handoff of the center to Hodges to provide even more opportunities for the adults and children in Jubilation as well as the surrounding community of Immokalee.

But times do change—not only in Collier County government over the last six years, but throughout the nation as a whole. Trust that may have been present in personal and business relationships was being replaced, in many cases, by fear and doubt.

During the next several months, our feelings were transformed from hope and excitement to despair and anxiety. The Collier County Department of Zoning and Land Development Review decided that it would not allow the simple "Letter Approval" transfer of ownership to take place. In order for the college to take title to the facility, we would have to start the laborious, expensive PUD process all over again, and address requirements for signage, landscaping, and parking in an entirely new plan. Hodges would have to plant several hundred bushes in multiple locations to buffer the "university building" from the residential community. Signage would have to be added to one parking lot stating, "Parking for residents only—no student parking" even though there were more than the required number of parking spaces. And maintenance of the landscaping along the entire exterior wall of the subdivision would have to be shifted from the Jubilation Community Homeowners' Association to Hodges University.

Our protests fell on deaf ears and we had no choice but to jump through hoops month after month, addressing new issues brought up by the department. In addition, the fact that a PUD Amendment was required would preclude the full Board of Collier County Commissioners from hearing our request until it was received and reviewed by the Collier County Planning Commission.

This would require more letters of explanation and continued reports about why this change of ownership would be beneficial to Immokalee. The process left Florence and me weary and in disbelief. Our original experience of building Jubilation itself had been a joy for us. Now we were forced to fight with all the resources we could muster.

We did get help from a long-time resident of Immokalee, Paul Midney, a friend of Harvest for Humanity for many years who served on the Collier County Planning Commission. He wrote strong letters of support for us and gave us much encouragement. Unfortunately, Paul was out of the country during the Collier County Planning Commission's final hearing and unable to vote. But another member of the planning commission, Brad Schiffer, stepped up to the plate and supported our efforts.

Finally, after several delays, on June 7, 2007, the Collier County Planning Commission had to spend nearly an entire day reviewing our "straightforward" request because county staff recommended that the project be denied, largely on the basis that a "college campus" was not appropriate for a "residential subdivision." For many months prior to the June 7th hearing, we were simply unable to convince county staff that the building would not be used as a "classic campus." Our position was that there would be only minor internal changes in use of the existing building with no negative impact on the existing residential community. At the June 7th hearing there were lengthy testimonies given by Hodges University representatives, Florence and me, and several Jubilation homeowners stating their desire for this new Hodges learning facility.

In her presentation to the planning commission, Florence came to tears when she tried to make sense of the obstructionist path that county staff had set us on after the years of dedication we had already contributed to Immokalee. My feelings, although I didn't express them as such, were mostly about anger

. . . anger about what should have been done in Immokalee to fight poverty even before Florence and I ever arrived there.

That day, June 7, 2007, at the Collier County Planning Commission, seven brave members voted to overturn the staff recommendation and sent our petition with their approval to the Collier County Board of Commissioners. Unfortunately, one planning commission member voted "no," which meant that we would not be able to appear on the board's "consent agenda." Instead, the entire county board would have the option of a full discussion of our petition. After thanking the members of the Collier County Planning Commission, we began preparations for the next battle.

Jim Coletta tried to reassure us that the rest of the board would positively receive our request, but again county staff tried to delay scheduling our petition. Finally, in July 2007, we were able to get our request on the Collier County's Board of Commissioners' agenda. We had started the approval process in September 2006 and it was now ten months later. This time period was the longest, most difficult time for Florence and me during our time in Immokalee. We felt more powerless than we ever had before. There was little we could to do ensure that the center would be used for one of its original purposes—to provide residents educational opportunities. We both hated the idea of leaving the building vacant but we knew we could no longer afford to keep it open.

Even as the day approached for the July board meeting, it was not clear how the board members would actually vote. We were told that the board generally does not overturn the recommendation of the planning commission, but that it could and occasionally did. Florence and I prayed that we would be able to accept the unintended consequences of leaving Immokalee with our Harvest Center closed and abandoned. It wasn't just about us or the center, but about so many people throughout

Immokalee and how they would be hurt. It was also about people outside of Immokalee who could continue to stereotype the town, saying things like, "You don't want to go there—it's poor; it's hopeless." It would confirm what the naysayers had said along, "See, it couldn't be done, not in Immokalee."

We didn't sleep well those nights even though we tried to continue to be positive. We even planned to have Harvest and Hodges attorneys attend the meeting. That way if we did receive approval, we could close on the property and transfer title that day.

On July 24, 2007, we were fortunate to have Jim Coletta presiding as chairman. We obtained a "time certain" for our hearing of 1:00 P.M., right after lunch. When the board reconvened at that time, Jim anticipated a quick approval. After all, we had submitted numerous reports, explanations, and resources, and a commitment by Hodges University to keep Jubilation secure and safe. Jim opened the meeting asking for a motion for approval of the project, but his request was promptly ignored by the other three board members present in person. The fifth board member, Tom Henning, was present by phone; he was on the East Coast after attending his mother's funeral a few days earlier.

My thoughts turned to my own mom and I felt her presence. She had passed on two years earlier, but she had always been anxious to hear from Florence and me about how our project was going in Immokalee. She was pleased with our work and how it positively affected so many lives. This wasn't surprising, you know, because one of her favorite movies was also . . . *It's a Wonderful Life*.

I was jolted back to reality when the attorney for Hodges was asked again by the board to make a presentation to justify the change in use and transfer in title. This was quite a shock as this material had been presented many times in the past.

What we didn't know, until that moment, was that the board was generally in favor of the project—until less than twenty-four hours before, when county planning staff apparently had the opportunity to instill new doubts about the transfer. Over the next full hour, Jubilation residents spoke on behalf of the project. Barb Cacchione was out of town that day, but had written an impassioned plea stating she believed that approving the transfer of ownership was the right thing to do. Terry McMahon assured everyone what a good neighbor Hodges would be.

Florence moved the audience with her explanation of why it was so important to bring this higher education opportunity to Immokalee. I spoke last, addressing the board about their upcoming vote. The board members had two options. One was to participate in this educational milestone that was badly needed in Immokalee. The other choice was to vote against it, leaving an abandoned building with no source of funding to keep it open.

As the time for the final vote approached, the three board members present said that they were inclined to vote against the project. Time stood still for a moment as I sat motionless. I saw much of what we worked for in Immokalee slipping through our fingers. Florence clutched my hand, tears in her eyes. We couldn't believe that our work was coming to such an abrupt and sad ending. With Jim Coletta shocked and speechless, a silence came over the room as we all waited.

Terry glanced at me in silent dismay. For our petition to be granted, we needed four out of five votes. Suddenly, the silence was broken by the voice on the phone conference call. Tom Henning spoke passionately. He said he had no doubt that Immokalee needed this facility and the board should not deny the community this opportunity. Once again I thought of my mom. Tom had just lost his mother, and yet here he was thinking of Immokalee and fighting for what it needed. Maybe it wasn't a coincidence I'd been thinking of my mother. Maybe her spirit had been with Tom while he listened to the proceedings from 1,000 miles away. Did she, in some way we couldn't understand, move him to speak so passionately? Was she another angel working on our behalf?

After Tom's unexpected interjection, we were surprised when suddenly another board member, Donna Fiala, said she would support it if Tom would. The remaining Board members, Frank Halas and Fred Coyle, finally agreed. Jim quickly asked for a motion, a vote, and it was unanimous—five to zero in our favor. All this happened in seven minutes from the time we first heard Tom's voice until we heard the vote. Florence and I refer to this as "the seven-minute miracle!"

Florence and I were spent, but we also rejoiced at the sudden turn of events. Jim recessed the meeting quickly, brought us to his conference room, and told us to take the time we needed to complete the closing. The paperwork went without a hitch.

In January 2008, the Hodges Learning Site at Jubilation opened with sixteen students, including Carmelita, who continued to work there as well. It quickly grew to full capacity and by September, was serving eighty students. That same month, the new iTech High School opened in Immokalee and Hodges rented two rooms for students to take college classes there. The iTech is a state-of-the-art facility for technical and vocational education, offering classes in nursing, computer graphics, hair design, car repair, and culinary services. About forty students attend Hodges at the iTech.

In March 2008 Hodges held a special celebration in Jubilation and honored us by renaming the Harvest Activity Center the Richard and Florence Nogaj Building. This marked the end of one stage of our journey. We would continue to work for Fair Food and immigration reform, and to share the Harvest for Humanity message with college students visiting Immokalee every spring.

Nearly nine years had passed since the rainy spring morning in Wheaton when I met a hitchhiker who would literally change my life. Through our early work with Habitat for Humanity, Florence and I gained many of the skills we would need to build Jubilation, create a living-wage farm, and make educational opportunities available to people in Immokalee and the surrounding areas. We didn't achieve all of our dreams—our initial goal of having employees being able to own the Harvest Farm wasn't met, and the Blueberry Store and Harvest Café did not turn out to be sustainable businesses.

Yet through our partnership and the help of dozens of give-back, community-minded people—and a few angels along the way—we did make a difference in Immokalee. Eighty-nine families now are living in safe, affordable housing they own, not rent, giving them stability and their children better opportunities for the future. The employees and farm workers there had, and have, jobs that paid decent, living wages. We developed and publicized the Fair Food concept, and helped raise the consciousness of thousands of people who otherwise might have been unaware of the needs of this community. With Hodges University we brought higher education opportunities to Immokalee and its residents so they can both continue to grow and thrive.

And for Florence and me, it truly has been the journey of a lifetime—although we wonder whether it's truly over. In late June 2007, we were in the office late packing up files and paperwork to prepare for the transfer of the center to Hodges University when Gloria Dominguez, one of our Jubilation homeowners, phoned and asked to meet with us.

Gloria, originally from the Bahamas, had worked as a teacher in Immokalee for many years. Soft-spoken and deeply spiritual, she would often visit us at the center and offer support and encouragement—especially during tough times. This time she said she felt compelled to have us join her for a simple but prayerful "Feast of Thanksgiving" to thank God for the work we had done and for the future. We had a short meal that evening (which was the last served at the Harvest Café) that included fruit, bread, and water. Afterwards she asked us to kneel on the floor, hold hands, and pray with her.

Gloria spoke softly but with certainty. "I believe God wants me to tell you that although your work in Immokalee is ending, God has even bigger plans for you in the future," she said.

Florence and I looked at each other in surprise. Gloria never knew the story of the hitchhiker. Was another angel in our midst? We'd have to wait and see.

PART III
THE CURRENT YEARS

Chapter Eleven

A CALL TO ACT

AFTER WE TRANSFERRED THE title for the Harvest Activity Center to Hodges University in 2007, the work that Florence and I had committed to in Immokalee was largely completed. It was time to move on . . . or was it? Some people had said that we had tried to perpetuate ourselves by doing something that counts. But what we wanted to do was bigger than that. We wanted to not only do something that counts, but something that would make a lasting difference.

The organizations that we founded and built are continuing to thrive under new leadership, and that gives us great comfort and satisfaction. The risks we took in the past are producing rewards in the improved quality of lives that have been positively affected by our work. We continue to believe in and work for (1) fair wages, (2) attainable home ownership, and (3) higher education. But there are other priorities for Florence and me—work that we have started and remains work in process.

Fair Food Movement

On a spring day in 2001, Florence and I met with Caroline Berver in Washington, DC. Caroline, one of Senator Bob Graham's staff members, was aware of the plight of the farm workers in Immokalee as she had already spoken with Greg Asbed, founder of the Coalition of Immokalee Workers (CIW). I had met Greg on one of our first visits to Immokalee, and he had suggested I contact Caroline and talk to her about my tax credit program idea back in 1999.

Since then, I'd begun to believe that not only did farm workers need to be paid a fair living wage but that growers needed to obtain a fair price for the food they brought to the marketplace as well. (In the coming years this problem would be further exacerbated by the government's passing of NAFTA, the North American Free Trade Agreement, and CAFTA, the Central America Free Trade Agreement, or what is referred to as "free trade" legislation. It may be "kind of free" for multinational corporations but it is costly for the rest of us.)

I had also come to the conclusion that the agricultural industry is "upside down." Almost all of the other industries in the United States operate as primarily "price-makers" for the product or services they provide, while the growers in Immokalee, for example, do the opposite. Many of those growers were "price-takers," meaning that whatever the market would pay, after the growers had expended their own funds for planting and harvesting, is what they would get—and it was usually a lower price than they expected.

During our first three years in Immokalee I had spent considerable time developing a proposal that would be similar to the Work Opportunity Tax Credit legislation already enacted by Congress. That legislation provided eligible employers with an incentive in the form of a tax credit for each Welfare-to-Work recipient they hired. In our case, I was proposing a tax credit for those growers that paid a living wage (about three or four dollars per hour above the minimum wage) to farm workers. These growers would be able to label, advertise, and market their produce as Fair Food. In turn, large buyers of produce would also be able to employ "cause-related marketing" campaigns that would let them market themselves as "Fair Food" companies.

The idea was to differentiate Fair Food from "commodity food" while asking consumers to pay a little more for safely-grown foods picked by workers paid living wages. The ramifications of this approach could be far-reaching; it could help eliminate poverty in agricultural communities like Immokalee, decrease illegal immigration related to agriculture because job turnover would be significantly reduced, and improve economic conditions for fruit and vegetable growers through increased margins. The process would allow living wages to become the standard through public support and the purchase of Fair Food in the market.

To sell this concept, though, Senator Graham's staffers needed to have a "sunset provision" in the legislation that would allow the tax credit to be temporary as Congress would probably not approve of a permanent tax credit. In order to accomplish that, a substantial advertising campaign would have to be undertaken and at least partially funded through a public/private partnership between industry and government. That campaign would educate consumers about Fair Food so that they could recognize and pay a little more for the produce grown by certified tax credit growers. Once Fair Food became popular and established with the buying public, the higher price that the grower would receive would allow him to pay his farm workers the higher wage without having to be subsidized by a government tax credit. This was the ultimate goal of the program.

That afternoon at Senator Graham's office, we talked for several hours, debating how to structure the bill. We all took copious notes and at the end of the meeting, Caroline promised to get back to us with questions. The next day she faxed us a three-page memo of questions; after talking with several of my colleagues, I faxed her back our answers. Our collaboration continued for several months as our hope for new legislation began to take shape.

And then it happened . . . 9/11. Overnight, priorities in Congress seemed to change dramatically. Although our legislation became lost in the intensity of the times, our commitment to the issue did not. Florence and I just decided to take a different course. We undertook a project that we hoped would substantiate our claim that the public would pay more for Fair Food if they understood its benefits, just as many consumers already paid more for organic food. Tom Obreza at IFAS helped us write a grant application to the Southern Region SARE Center to examine this question. The grant application was approved in early 2002.

The study was designed to test the viability of a "differentiated" label that singled out, in our case, Harvest for Humanity Blueberries from the rest as (1) USA-grown, and (2) picked by workers paid a "Living Wage." The project involved developing and administering surveys to grocery shoppers and was conducted during May 2002 and May 2003 in southwest Florida.

Depending on the results of the surveys, the project could set the stage for implementation of a "Living Wage" campaign or a "Fair Food America" campaign throughout the agricultural industry. The campaigns could include certification of growers; local, regional, and/or national ad campaigns; and enlistment of retail grocery chains at the national level to provide "Living Wage/Fair Food America Produce" sections in their stores.

The results from the surveys in both 2002 and 2003 found a label stating that produce was grown and picked in the USA by workers paid a living wage was important to nearly eight out of ten shoppers. Consumers seemed to sense that this kind of label would help introduce fairness in the industry. The survey results also found that:

- 75 percent of those surveyed said that having "living wage" on the label was important to them.
- 75 percent said they would be inclined to shop at grocery stores that carry "living wage" produce. In fact, 87 percent of female shoppers agreed with this statement.
- 82 percent of those surveyed would pay 5 percent more for "living wage" produce grown in the USA on living wage farms.
- Almost two-thirds of those surveyed believed that both the grower and retailer are responsible for preventing substandard working conditions.
- About two-thirds of those surveyed would support a federal tax credit for growers who paid farm workers a living wage.

The results suggested that many consumers are prepared to change their shopping habits to help eliminate poverty among farm workers. What was also important is that there seemed to be a distinct advantage for those retailers who would promote and sell "living wage" USA-grown produce. This represents an opportunity for those stores to gain a competitive advantage over other produce chains, as the large majority of the consumers surveyed indicated they would gravitate to such stores and, therefore, be willing to pay more for produce certified to be grown and picked by fairly-paid farm workers.

The study, entitled "Test Marketing of New Label in Southwest Florida for USA Grown/Living Wage Produce," can be reviewed on the SARE website at www.sare.org. Click on "Project Reports" and do a search for "Living Wage Produce."

The year 2002 also gave Florence and me the opportunity to introduce our ideas about living wages and Fair Food at conferences throughout the country. In June 2002 I spoke at a conference hosted by DePaul University in Chicago entitled "City in a Garden: Producing and Consuming Food in the New Millennium." I was a member of a panel called "Farms and Farm Workers," moderated by Professor Lincoln Johnson of the University of Notre Dame. (A group of students from Notre Dame had previously participated in its "Alternative Spring Break" program and had spent a week in Immokalee.)

In November 2002 Florence and I spoke at the Conference on Ecolabels and the Greening of the Food Market held at Tufts University in Boston. I presented a paper on our new food label entitled "Grown and Picked in the USA by Workers Paid a Living Wage." An excerpt from the abstract for the paper read:

> Harvest Farm uses an ecolabel for its high-quality early blueberries. The label includes characteristics such as local origin, pesticide-free, use of integrated pest management (IPM) procedures, and social justice. Harvest Farm workers are paid a living wage starting at $8.50 per hour. New marketing associations and partnerships with retailers are being

cultivated that emphasize the label while telling the
Harvest story.

The concept of a new ecolabel and the marketing of Fair
Food were beginning to take shape. In January 2003, another
good friend, Professor Camilo Azacarate, organized a special
agricultural meeting, the Southwest Florida Agricultural
Forum, at Florida Gulf Coast University in Fort Myers. The
forum was a one-day event designed to bring stakeholders from
the southwest Florida agriculture industry—growers, farm
workers, retailers, consumer groups, researchers, community
leaders, government officials, and political representatives—
together to propose ideas to address the current crisis of
agricultural produce. Leading national experts addressed issues with participants and explored marketing alternatives to
help consumers differentiate the value of US-grown produce
as not only healthier but also as an environmentally friendly
and socially responsible choice.

The goals of the forum were: (1) to fact-find regarding the
pros and cons of creating a Fair Food label for agricultural produce in southwest Florida; (2) to create a task force to examine
possible implementation steps; and (3) to increase the quality
of the communication between different stakeholders. The
forum initiated a conversation between industry stakeholders
exploring different marketing approaches to differentiate produce and created a ten-person task force to continue the work
started during the forum.

The task force met periodically over the next several years,
but momentum waned for a variety of reasons. One of the most
important reasons, in my opinion, was the lack of willingness
on the government's part to participate in a private/public
partnership with the growers. Legislators in general did not
seem interested in the possibility of entering the partnerships

necessary for struggling small growers, farm workers, and residents of our nation's poorer communities.

As we move into the second decade of this millennium, we have renewed hope that we will be able to "restart" and obtain political support for programs like Fair Food and provide tax credits to growers who pay living wages. There is much that needs to be done, including massive education and advertising programs funded by the government and designed to benefit the poor.

Immigration Reform

Another issue that is close to our hearts and that Florence and I continue to work for is immigration reform. Back in the 60s, I was part of a group of civil rights activists who worked with Mexican families who labored in the vegetable fields in western DuPage County. That was my first introduction to immigration issues. Later, with Habitat for Humanity in DuPage County, many of the families who applied for and were selected to own Habitat homes were of Mexican descent; some were still involved in farm work.

In the early 90s, I met and became good friends with Luis Pelayo, president of the Hispanic Council of Chicago, and began working with the Hispanic Council to help improve conditions for Hispanic families. In September, 1996 Florence and I attended a gala benefit and awards ceremony in Chicago where the Hispanic Council gave me an award for the civic work I helped initiate on behalf of Hispanic people.

Our work with Harvest in Immokalee brought us to an even deeper understanding of the plight of the migrant farm workers. This experience, combined with our involvement and friendship with the Hispanic Council in Chicago, educated us about the poverty that people were experiencing in countries like Mexico and Guatemala and their struggle for a better life.

Florence and I became involved because we thought we could make a difference. We already had a platform for reaching the public through our work with Habitat for Humanity and Harvest for Humanity. By making presentations to as many groups as we could, we could raise people's consciousness levels and lobby our government officials for action on badly needed immigration reform.

In January 2007, we traveled to Washington DC with a group of immigration reform supporters to meet with Senator Dick Durbin's staff and deliver a personal letter to as many senators and representatives as we could. I wore the lapel pin I'd received from the Hispanic Council more than ten years prior. Our group included Margaret Carrasco, president of the Casa Mexiquense in Waukegan, Illinois, and Luis Pelayo, president of the Hispanic Council of Chicago.

We met with Reema Dodin, one of Senator Durbin's office staff, and spent the next two days seeing as many senators, representatives, and their staff that we could. We hand-delivered a letter requesting action on immigration reform legislation signed by twenty Latino organizations to those officials we couldn't meet with. The letter asked legislators to resurrect the McCain-Kennedy initiative that was introduced on May 12, 2005, and was languishing without action (as it still is as of today). We hoped that our senators from Illinois, Senator Durbin and Senator Obama, would step forward and restart the process.

The letter included the following language:

Dear Congressional Member:

We appreciate the opportunity to bring to your attention, through this letter, the position of the undersigned regarding the immigration controversy and upcoming consideration of bills in Congress.

Last week, members of Congress reintroduced the AgJobs Act for farm workers and their families. Even with passage of this bill the solution, however, to the status of the remaining nine million undocumented majorities would not be addressed. Immigration reform should not be a piece-meal project. It needs to be based on a comprehensive earned legalization process, which is not blanket amnesty. It should leave nobody out or set any preference of some folks over the other.

Comprehensive immigration legislation would:

- *Encompass the DREAM ACT (public college access at in-state tuition rates for not-legally-documented students that have graduated from a state school)*

- *Include the AGJOBS ACT (geared to agricultural workers only)*

- *Resolve the legal situation of the undocumented majority*

- *Improve border security by allowing the border patrol to concentrate on drug smugglers and criminals, instead of people looking for a job to feed their families.*

Mexican workers represent an economic asset and not a liability to this country. They provide the workforce that keeps our industries competitive in a global market. Lack of economic opportunities to sustain their families, not criminal intent, is why people are looking for work. (Perhaps in the future, a Marshall Plan for Mexico can become a legislative agenda item with far-reaching positive ramifications.)

Comprehensive immigration legislation would require:

- *Creating a new immigration category (H5A and H5B)*

- *Paying a fine for entering without inspection*

- *Documenting a productive five year US employment record*

- *Being up-to-date on income taxes.*

Lack of economic opportunities to sustain their families, not criminal intent, is why people are looking for work. No one should die looking for a job. We need immigration reform now.

Sincerely,

The Chicago Metropolitan Alliance of Latino Organizations

After three days of pounding the hallways of Congress, we returned home empty-handed and without encouragement. We received no promises from the legislators and staff we spoke with. Since then, I have continued to speak to as many groups as I can on the subject, especially about the terrible, inhumane fear that good, law-abiding and hard-working families suffer at the hands of some officials because of indiscriminate raids. These families are forced to live in the shadows, in a state of constant fear for the lives of their children and themselves. This is not the America that so many of us have fought for. Thankfully many of us are still waging the battle for badly-needed immigration reform legislation.

I am always taken aback by the term "illegal alien." Does the word "alien" refer to an extraterrestrial being as Webster suggests? Though not legally documented, these folks are not criminals. Crossing the border without documents carries but one penalty and that is deportation by the federal authorities. It is a civil offense, not a criminal act.

Yet many people are misinformed about immigration reform. Take the term "amnesty," which means to pardon without consequence. Immigration reform advocates aren't asking for amnesty; the proper term is "earned legalization," which most of the public favors. Earned legalization means creating a path to legal status that would include living here for several years, paying fines, learning English, being of good character, and having no criminal record.

People come to the United States to work. Even by closing the border we only address about 50 percent of undocumented residents as about half are here with visa "overstays" and did not come across the border. The 9/11 terrorists were all overstayers and none came across the Mexican border.

A typical immigrant contributes about $100,000 more resources to the country in his lifetime than he uses. Over $20 billion is collected from immigrants and sent to Social Security, and none of this will be returned to unauthorized workers. The federal government relies on these funds to pay benefits to the rest of us, and focusing our efforts on deportation is ineffective and expensive. According to an August 2009 report issued by the Cato Institute of Washington, DC, immigration reform that includes legalization would yield a net benefit of $180 billion over ten years, while enforcement efforts alone would cost $80 billion.

As I've seen firsthand, our farming economy relies on these "illegal" immigrants. Most agricultural employers in Florida hire workers with social security cards that cannot be accurately verified. If we deport these agricultural workers, all of us will be severely impacted. We must not become dependent on foreign food of which only 1 percent is inspected. We must support safe and healthy American-grown Fair Food, which does mean higher wages and higher prices.

Yet in the agriculture industry, wages for farm workers are not being increased because our society pays the least percentage of income for fresh fruit and vegetables than any other industrialized country in the world. This situation was worsened by NAFTA and CAFTA, when many tomato farms owned by multi-national corporations moved south of the border to pay their workers lower wages.

In Mexico, 52 percent of the 100 million people live in poverty and make less than $2.00 per day. If you lived in conditions like these and your family had no food, wouldn't you risk your life by crossing the border to work in a job that nobody else wants that will keep your family from starving to death? The people who come here are courageous, young, and hard-working—and I know that firsthand. The many people Florence and I have met and come to know work extremely hard and don't deserve the worst that America has to offer—living in the shadows and in fear, being stopped and asked for documents without cause.

Until Congress passes comprehensive immigration reform, I will continue to speak whenever asked and take every opportunity to educate the public about this critical issue. The battle may not be won as yet, but it is not over.

Passing the Torch

Florence and I believe that part of our work is to raise public consciousness about the issues affecting poverty-stricken families. We have made hundreds of presentations to civic, religious, educational, and social groups about our work, and what people can do to make a difference. One of our favorite aspects of this work is working with college students.

Every year since 2002, Florence and I eagerly anticipate the arrival of the "Alternative Spring Break" (ASB) students to Immokalee from various colleges and universities. Most students come from Midwestern or Eastern schools; on the average, each spring about a dozen students from ten different schools spend their spring break working with the less fortunate in Immokalee rather than partying on the beaches of Fort Lauderdale. The visits are staggered, depending on each school's spring break schedule.

They help teach younger children in the grade schools, work in the soup kitchen in the Guadalupe Center, and assist people like Jim Kean, a full-time volunteer there for many years. They sleep at the Immokalee homeless shelter in very humble surroundings, and learn firsthand about poverty in Immokalee. Each group generally sets aside one day for the

Harvest for Humanity experience. Early in the morning Florence and I meet and greet the students, have breakfast with them when we can, and lead a three-hour seminar about Harvest for Humanity and Jubilation on subjects like planned neighborhood developments, sustainability, and community building. We also introduce them to concepts like living wages and Fair Food and talk about the changes we think are necessary to alleviate the wage and price problems we've experienced firsthand in the fresh fruit and vegetable farming industry.

After lunch, the students get to meet the farm workers and spend the rest of the afternoon learning about farming and assisting the workers in their tasks. We've heard from most of the students after they returned to their college campuses, and have found that many were planning to join organizations like the Peace Corps or AmeriCorps, or to dedicate their lives to help make a difference in the lives of those less fortunate either here in the United States or abroad.

In February 2009 Florence and I greeted twelve students from Georgetown University, located in Washington, DC. I sensed that there was still excitement lingering from the January inauguration. After brief introductions in the parking lot, I asked the students to wait. In a booming voice I said, "Before we go in and get started I need you to answer one question. Please raise your hand if you did NOT attend Barack Obama's inauguration."

They all looked at each other in surprise, and no one raised their hand. "Okay," I exclaimed. "It's good to know you are all civically engaged. Now we can get started!" That morning was filled with even more energy and enthusiasm than usual.

Florence and I will continue to return to Immokalee every year and welcome new students as they arrive for their Alternative Spring Break week. Sharing our experiences with them has created lasting memories for Florence and me, and we believe that it has helped create a better future for the students—and the lives they will touch—as well.

We've had dozens of appreciative notes and cards from dozens of students since 2002, and have kept their heartfelt letters. *"You have motivated my life and studies in truly an amazing way! Thank you both." "We learned an incredible amount about the situation of the migrant farm worker." "We were inspired by the people of your organization." "Thank you for allowing us to have this opportunity." "Thank you for teaching us about the injustices of the world."*

And finally: *"You really stirred so many thoughts and ideas . . . the two of you are shining examples to society. We wish more people would take their blessings and make a difference. Hopefully, we will be able to do for the community, but of course on a smaller scale, what Harvest for Humanity has done. You have created hope."*

We are all angels with one wing—all we have to do is join together to fly.

Afterword
Making a Difference:
What You Can Do

IT IS MY HOPE that you will be inspired to make a difference in the world. There are countless ways you can get involved, but the following organizations have touched Florence and me in our journey. We have a special place in our hearts for them, and if you decide to get involved, we hope you'll start with one (or more!) of the groups listed here.

International/Outside the United States

- To learn more about Habitat for Humanity's "Vacation with a Purpose" or "Global Village Program," contact Habitat for Humanity International, www.habitat.org. E-mail gv@habitat.org. Phone 800-422-4828. Street address: 121 Habitat Street Americus, GA, 31709.
- To learn more about helping to build homes in the USA or abroad with the "Global Builders Program," contact The Fuller Center, visit www.fullercenter.org. E-mail through website. Phone 229-924-2900. Street address: 701 S. Martin Luther King, Jr. Drive, Americus, GA, 31719.

Greater Chicago/Wheaton, Illinois

- If you are interested in working with the Hispanic community in the Chicago area, contact The Hispanic Council (Luis Pelayo, president), e-mail Hispanicouncil@aol.com. Phone 708-222-8422. Street address: 2127 S. Lombard Avenue, Suite 202, Cicero, IL 60804.
- For those who want to help build a house in DuPage County, Illinois, contact DuPage Habitat for Humanity (Sara Brachle, executive director), www.dupagehabitat. org. E-mail through website. Phone 630-510-3737. Street address: 213 S. Wheaton Avenue, Wheaton, IL 60187.
- The People's Resource Center offers a variety of volunteer opportunities. PRC runs a food bank and clothing connection, provides emergency assistance, and helps individuals and families improve their literacy, learn computer and technology skills, and attain employment, as well as running the PRC Arts Studio. Visit www.peoplesrc.org or e-mail through the website. Phone 630-682-5402. Street address: 201 S. Naperville Road, Wheaton, IL 60187.

Fort Myers/Immokalee, Florida

- If you want to help improve opportunities for children and create better lives for families, contact the Quality Life Center, www.qualitylifecenter.org or e-mail through website. Phone 239-334-2797. Street address: 3210 Dr. Martin Luther King, Jr. Boulevard, Fort Myers, FL 33916.
- For those interested in improving the plight of farm workers contact the Coalition of Immokalee Workers, www.ciw-online.org. E-mail workers@ciw-online.org. Phone 239-657-8311. Mailing address: P.O. Box 603, Immokalee, FL 34143.

- If you're interested in promoting the Fair Food movement, contact the Alliance for Fair Food, www.allianceforfairfood. org. E-mail info@allianceforfairfood.org. Phone 212-253-1761. Street address: 1107 New Market Road, Immokalee, FL 34142.
- If you're interested in working with low-income residents in Immokalee, contact Guadalupe Social Services, www. guadalupess.org. E-mail through website. Phone 239-657-6242. Street address: 211 S. Ninth Street, Immokalee, Fl 34142.

Throughout the United States

- If you want to work for social justice, contact The Sider Center on Ministry and Public Policy, www.esa-online.org, which offers a variety of volunteer opportunities. E-mail through website. Phone 484-384-2990. Street address: 6 E. Lancaster Avenue, Wynnewood, PA 19096.
- If you want to work for social justice, contact Dr. Tony Campolo at the Evangelical Association for the Promotion of Education, www.tonycampolo.org. One of the organization's priorities is working with the poor in Haiti, especially children. E-mail through website. Phone 610-341-5962. Street address: 1300 Eagle Road, St. Davids, PA 19087.
- For those interested in joining the campaign for meaningful immigration reform, contact the National Immigration Forum, www.immigrationforum.org. E-mail through website. Phone 202-347-0040. Street address: 50 F. Street NW, Suite 300, Washington, DC 20001.
- To contact the White House and let your voice be heard, visit the website at www.whitehouse.gov. E-mail through website. Phone the comments line at 202-456-6213 or switchboard at 202-456-1414. Street address: The White

House, 1600 Pennsylvania Avenue NW, Washington, DC 20500.

- To contact your state senator or representative, visit www. congress.org for names and contact information. Or phone the US Capital Switchboard at 202-224-3121.

GET IN TOUCH

Has this book inspired you to make a difference? I'd love to hear how you've helped make the world—or your community—a better place, and welcome your comments, thoughts, and ideas about our story and our ongoing work. Contact me at dicknogaj@gmail.com or visit www.dontretiregetinspired.com to get in touch.

—**Dick Nogaj**

To order additional copies of this title call:
1-877-421-READ (7323)
or please visit our Web site at
www.winepressbooks.com

If you enjoyed this quality custom-published book,
drop by our Web site for more books and information.

www.winepressgroup.com

"Your partner in custom publishing."

For further information please visit our website:
www.dontretiregetinspired.com